T0231113

UX STYLE FRAMEWORKS

UX Style Frameworks: Creating Collaborative Standards is a practical guide for the hands-on creation of a Style Framework. This new and collaborative documentation format combines different departments' standards and style guides into a single, unified, and accessible source for all employees. Marti Gold defines Style Frameworks for web and user experience designers, showing what and how much information goes into a Style Framework.

As UX designers and creative directors are charged with ensuring a business's web and mobile output are in line with branding standards, the unification of style guides, code libraries, and pattern libraries is an important aspect to dissolving "design silos" and creating a unified brand. Each section of the book will identify the current pain points and common internal practices that result in standards documents being ignored and eventually becoming obsolete. *UX Style Frameworks* provide solutions for creating Style Frameworks that evolve to keep standards current, ultimately resulting in more cohesive brand and product designs.

Key features:

- Offers a fully functional companion website with a complete Style Framework, showing all the examples featured in the book, and available for download so that users can start their own Style Frameworks.

- A special section includes information about addressing company politics and policies to help readers navigate those murky waters to ensure buy-in and establishment of Style Frameworks.

- Includes detailed descriptions of the elements within a Style Framework, how those elements should be defined and presented, and gives the reader examples of the different ways Style Frameworks can be incorporated into their existing workflows.

Marli Gold is a Dallas-based UX/Creative Director. She is currently the Managing Director of User Experience for Tonic3 (tonic3.com), the UX division of W3 (w3americas.com) a global interactive agency whose clients include Citi, Accenture, Disney, and Intuit. Formerly Creative Director at Travelocity, her extensive award-winning portfolio includes work for Expedia, AT&T, Best Buy, the MGM Grand Hotel, and many other internationally recognized brands.

UX STYLE FRAMEWORKS

CREATING COLLABORATIVE STANDARDS

Marti Gold

CRC Press
Taylor & Francis Group
Boca Raton   London   New York

CRC Press is an imprint of the
Taylor & Francis Group, an informa business

CRC Press
Taylor & Francis Group
6000 Broken Sound Parkway NW, Suite 300
Boca Raton, FL 33487-2742

© 2016 Taylor & Francis

CRC Press is an imprint of the Taylor & Francis Group, an informa business

This book contains information obtained from authentic and highly regarded sources. Reasonable efforts have been made to publish reliable data and information, but the author and publisher cannot assume responsibility for the validity of all materials or the consequences of their use. The authors and publishers have attempted to trace the copyright holders of all material reproduced in this publication and apologize to copyright holders if permission to publish in this form has not been obtained. If any copyright material has not been acknowledged please write and let us know so we may rectify in any future reprint.

Except as permitted under U.S. Copyright Law, no part of this book may be reprinted, reproduced, transmitted, or utilized in any form by any electronic, mechanical, or other means, now known or hereafter invented, including photocopying, microfilming, and recording, or in any information storage or retrieval system, without written permission from the publishers.

For permission to photocopy or use material electronically from this work, please access www.copyright.com (http://www.copyright.com/) or contact the Copyright Clearance Center, Inc. (CCC), 222 Rosewood Drive, Danvers, MA 01923, 978-750-8400. CCC is a not-for-profit organization that provides licenses and registration for a variety of users. For organizations that have been granted a photocopy license by the CCC, a separate system of payment has been arranged.

Trademark Notice: Product or corporate names may be trademarks or registered trademarks, and are used only for identification and explanation without intent to infringe.

Library of Congress Cataloging in Publication Data
A catalog record for this books has been requested.

ISBN: 978-1-138-85647-9 (hbk)
ISBN: 978-1-138-85648-6 (pbk)
ISBN: 978-1-315-71961-0 (ebk)

Typeset in Trade Gothic by Marti Gold
Cover design by Marti Gold
Cover image @dariusl/Stockfresh

Visit the Taylor & Francis Web site at http://www.taylorandfrancis.com and the CRC Press Web site at http://www.crcpress.com

To Nathan, Ellis, Andrew, Lauren, and Lindsay.

SINCERE THANKS TO...

- My editor, Lauren Penn, who caught every Oxford Comma that I missed.

- My technical editor, Kip Read, who taught me that books should be organized very differently from presentations.

- My first-round reviewers, Eric Reiss and Russ Unger, for asking some tough questions which made this book stronger.

- My colleagues, Brian Sullivan and Adam Polansky, who convinced me it was time to begin speaking and writing.

- My boss, Joe Edwards, who should win awards for being the Best Boss Ever.

- And finally, all my direct reports—both past and present. I learned more from you than you will ever know.

UX STYLE FRAMEWORKS
TABLE OF CONTENTS

Introduction

A Day in the Life of a UX Style Framework

Creating a UX Style Framework

Table of Contents *continued*

Sample Content

Supplemental Materials

FOREWORD

A few years ago, while attending the BigDesign Conference in Dallas, I had the opportunity to hear noted usability expert Jared Spool's keynote address. At that time, I was the Creative Director for a large online travel site. For the previous six months, a great deal of my effort had been devoted to the completion of our company's new corporate style guide. I was quite convinced this new style guide was critically important and had trumpeted its benefits to the entire company. It was going to minimize churn, give us a more consistent user experience, save development time, and solve countless other issues we were facing at that time.

However, a few minutes before Jared's presentation, my colleague Adam Polansky, the head of our Information Architecture department, walked up to me and quietly said, "I'm afraid this keynote is going to make you very angry."

I was somewhat perplexed by this statement and asked, "Why?" Adam replied, "Well, I've heard Jared give this particular talk before. Just trust me—he's going to make you mad."

A few minutes later, the presentation started. Jared was breezing along, as informative and entertaining as always. But about halfway through, he began talking about something called "Rules Based Design," which he stated was usually presented in the form of a style guide.

Then, in front of all my direct reports, colleagues, and my boss (the person who approved all the funding and resources necessary for me to continue my style guide project), Jared said…

"In Rules-Based design, Style Guides are created so that *unintentional* designers can *accidentally* create great designs. The problem is that design Style Guides never work. People stop using them."
– Jared Spool

Well, from that point until the end of his speech, I was sitting quietly, pretending to be polite and pay attention. But behind that mask I looked just like this kid.

I kept thinking, "Surely, a renowned expert like Jared Spool did not mean *my* style guide. My work was going to be used for years and was going to save my company millions of dollars."

© Voyagerix / Fotolia

I couldn't stop thinking about his speech the rest of the weekend. When I returned to the office on Monday, my attitude could best be described as, "I'll show him!" Whenever anyone asked about the BigDesign keynote, I explained that while Jared is indeed entertaining, he makes his living speaking about UX rather than actually doing it. So in this instance, he is apparently simply too far removed from the real world to recognize his error. I reinforced my position by showing examples of style guides from other large corporations who also understood the importance of standards work—all of us could not possibly be wrong. I remained very passionate and, after this minor bump in the road, our work continued on schedule.

Not long afterward, we finally launched our new Online Style Guide. It included everything our company needed in order to build and maintain a consistent brand and user experience for our website: grids, modules, buttons, interactions, colors... you name it. Everyone was given access to it, and I received numerous emails congratulating me on the launch, marveling at the depth of information presented, how wonderful it looked, and how useful it was going to be.

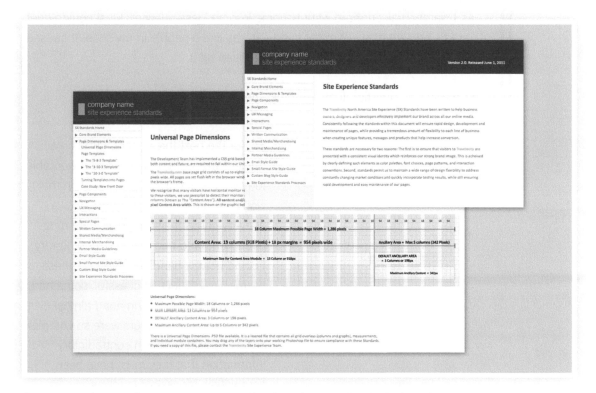

Screenshots from my first enterprise-level online Style Guide, right after its launch

Everything went very smoothly...for about three months. That's when the first exception requests started. At first they were innocent enough. But as my team continued to try and enforce our standards, stakeholders who did not like the answer "no" began entering visual design changes into our company's development bug tracking system. It had only taken them three months to realize that "bugs" were forwarded straight to development, bypassing the design team that was stopping their changes.

Within eight months, the first non-compliant page appeared on the site. Soon, there was another, and then another. Finally, only 18 months after its initial launch, my Style Guide was basically nothing but an outdated relic. Although it was quoted every now and then by someone trying to win an argument, all the problems it was supposed to fix— the endless debates, lack of consistency, and one-off code solutions—were back.

As I watched all our hard work become less and less relevant, I just couldn't get Jared's presentation out of my mind—it was like a pebble in my shoe. It caused me physical pain to admit it, but he had been right.

However, the question that burned in me was, *"Why?"*

So, for the next three years, I was on a quest. I was determined to find a workable format for standards documentation that would not eventually fall apart. I looked at every corporate style guide, branding document, and interaction pattern library I could get my hands on. Some of these seemed to be quite successful, some had been released and fallen apart almost immediately, while others were so complex and filled with so much contradictory information that they must have been completely impossible to follow.

After three years of evaluating different formats and examples, I began to realize that what was needed was not a style guide with carefully documented standards and template details, but a style *framework*: a rock-solid, base set of standards to ensure consistency that was stripped of complex, overly prescriptive elements. Something that would encourage new UX design solutions rather than hinder them. Something that could be easily maintained, and would evolve as sites and applications grew and as technologies changed.

UX Style Frameworks provide a single, unified source to locate visual, interaction, and development requirements gathered from multiple departments—Marketing, User Experience and Engineering. They eliminate conflicting information between those groups, are easy to maintain, and provide company-wide access to this important information.

Creating a UX Style Framework is not nearly as daunting as it may sound. If you have current standards documentation, you probably have most of the information already assembled. The upcoming chapters present a step-by-step guide to define the requirements of a good UX Style Framework, as well as all the information needed for you to create and effectively maintain one within your organization.

Some of these concepts are going to seem self-evident; some will seem unlikely; and some may seem downright controversial. But as you read, you will quickly begin to see how combining each department's separate standards into a single, collaborative repository may be the easiest, yet most dramatically impactful step you can take to improve the quality and decrease the development time of your applications.

After reading this book, I hope you discover that a UX Style Framework can provide the consistency your applications need, while remaining both collaborative and flexible. Most importantly, they do not lead to "Rules-based" design—and the inevitable obsolescence of overly-prescriptive documentation.

WHAT IS A UX STYLE FRAMEWORK?

Whenever I do a presentation on this topic, inevitably one of the first questions is, "How do UX Style Frameworks differ from regular style guides or pattern libraries?"

While a UX Style Framework does include much of the same content as its traditional counterparts, the presentation and organization of this content, as well as the processes surrounding the daily use and maintenance of the framework, are vastly different.

This chapter will introduce the major features of a UX Style Framework and some of the unique processes which differentiate it from traditional documentation. As we delve into more concrete details in subsequent chapters, these distinctions will become clearer. But for now, lets take a high-level look at the similarities and differences.

UX STYLE FRAMEWORKS: AN OVERVIEW

As you are probably aware, most company standards are split across multiple documents, with each one supported and maintained by a different department. It is not difficult to see how this structure evolved—marketing departments rarely need to include information on "required form field error states" in their brand guidelines, and developers could not care less if those brand guidelines specify black & white photography rather than full color images. However, other items, such as your brand's base colors and fonts, are normally defined in all these sources. As you will discover in an upcoming chapter, trying to define the same standard across multiple documents inevitably leads to conflicts—and huge problems.

Conversely, attempting to compile the full depth of detail needed by production designers and developers into one standards document is folly as well. Such a document will quickly grow so large and complex that finding and understanding a specific item becomes impossible.

UX Style Frameworks address this dilemma by providing a single source which presents each standard on an individual page, giving details on its use and construction, and consolidating all necessary links to that standard's production assets, research, and code.

This ensures a UX Style Framework is usable by everyone; from your most non-technical employees to your most senior designers and developers.

In addition to providing a single, easily searchable area to consolidate your standards, UX Style Frameworks provide a forum for open communication and collaboration between departments. This transparency will expose, and eventually eliminate, the conflicts between the various standard sets, as well as distribute the workload associated with the framework's ongoing maintenance.

As you will discover while reading this book, a single cross-departmental source with distributed ownership and transparent communications is the key to effective standards. Everyone in your company must be able to quickly access your standards, understand them, find the information or files they need, and feel free to suggest changes and improvements.

SIMILARITIES TO TRADITIONAL STANDARDS DOCUMENTATION

To better illustrate how this is accomplished, let's first take a quick look at some of the items included in traditional standards documentation which will be rolled into a UX Style Framework.

Similarities to Marketing Brand Guidelines

UX Style Frameworks will cover information on the proper presentation of your brand. This includes items such as: Details on the use of logos and the location of approved logo artwork; Complete typography rules for styling text; Formulas for all approved brand colors and gradients; Approved icons, photography, and illustration styles.

Similarities to Copy/Content Strategy Style Guides

In addition to visual styling, the framework will provide information on copy and content guidelines. Some examples are: The proper formatting, spelling and use of registration marks for all company brand names; Rules for consistent formatting of special data (dates, times, prices); Grammar rules and company approved spelling of common words or phrases (i.e. use of the "Oxford comma", "email" vs. "e-mail", "Log In" vs "Login").

Similarities to User Experience Pattern Libraries

The framework will also include details on tested interaction patterns and the rules on when to use each one, along with examples of approved visual styling. This includes: All approved interactions from simple buttons to complex show-hide solutions; Proper form formatting and error handling; Instructions on when and how to use each pattern.

Similarities to Development Presentation-Layer Toolkits

A UX Style Framework will present examples, as well as code snippets and/or links to approved code repositories, for many common presentation-layer interactions. This may include: The definition of page grids; Module behaviors when displayed in responsive layouts; Definitions for many reusable interactive elements.

DIFFERENCES FROM TRADITIONAL STANDARDS DOCUMENTATION

Conversely, much of the content, formatting and processes surrounding the use and creation of traditional standards documentation are the root causes of their eventual demise. UX Style Frameworks are quite different from traditional docs in the following areas:

Provides a Single, Cross-Departmental Source to Eliminate Conflicts

Having the same standard defined by multiple groups inevitably leads to conflicting specifications. With no ability to determine which specification is definitive, the user will reference the most convenient source—which may or may not be correct. By having every department's standards referenced in one place, these discrepancies can be spotted quickly and reconciled.

Creates a Common Vocabulary Company-Wide

Multiple standards also result in each department adopting multiple words to describe the same interaction or element. Confusion will be unavoidable if the marketing specs define a "lightbox", while designers discuss "overlays", and developers reference "modals". Style Frameworks ensure that all team members use the same vocabulary when speaking to one another.

Permits Cross-Departmental Ownership

Because multiple departments share ownership of the framework, each standard has the benefit of being fully vetted by the appropriate subject matter experts within your company. For example, your accessibility team may discover that marketing's proposed button colors are not WCAG compliant. Shared ownership allows potential problems such as this to surface quickly, allowing the entire group to find a solution before the standard is pushed into development.

Creates Completely Transparent Decision-Making Processes

By including an open discussion forum on each standard's page, debates on any standard's effectiveness, technical feasibility, change requests, and resulting decisions become completely transparent. This removes the risk that any single person or group can control the standards, and eliminates the complaint "we weren't consulted in the decision-making process."

A CRITICAL DIFFERENCE: UX STYLE FRAMEWORKS DEFINE ONLY "BUILDING BLOCK" ELEMENTS AND INTERACTIONS

Traditional standards are frequently overly-prescriptive. Many not only define core elements, but are expanded to include detailed specifications for large widgets, templates and sometimes even entire pages. This tendency to over-specify is grounded in the noble intention of ensuring consistency for end-users as well as reducing development time with reusable code.

Sadly, as you will see in upcoming chapters, over-specification invariably leads to design and development modifications to address unique business requirements. The result? The exact opposite of the original intent – inconsistent user experiences and one-off code solutions.

Style Frameworks define only basic elements and interactions for your application or site, allowing your product managers and designers to determine how to best arrange those elements to address each unique business requirement and user story most effectively.

By limiting your standards to only core elements and interactions, you give your stakeholders, designers and developers the freedom to arrange those elements into optimum interface solutions for your end-users. Prototyping and testing become easier; site-wide consistency and learnability are maintained; reusable code libraries which speed development become stable; quality assurance bugs decrease.

While it may seem counter-intuitive, the best way to ensure all the benefits of standards-based development is to *minimize and simplify* the items which are actually defined as standards.

© Elenathewise / Fotolia

WHO SHOULD ACCESS YOUR UX STYLE FRAMEWORK?

© deandrobot / Stockfresh

Ideally, your new UX Style Framework will sit outside the corporate firewall so it is available to anyone who needs current information on your standards. This includes vendors, partners, advertisers, and employees without access to your virtual private network.

While you may be reluctant to place company-specific information on an external server, virtually none of the information within a UX Style Framework is truly proprietary. After all, if someone can see your website or application, just a few seconds viewing the source with Chrome Developer Tools will reveal pretty much everything. Because of this, you may find the benefits of protecting your framework with a simple password and placing it outside your firewall for easy access by vendors and partners far outweighs the downsides.

However, even if you plan to have your UX Style Framework password protected, your company may not want to display certain types of information which are indeed critical for the framework to function properly. This information might include links to internal assets, employee names and valid email addresses, active discussions, or change requests.

To solve this particular problem, reach out to your development team. They can normally write a script to run each evening, creating a duplicate of the day's updated content. This data feed can be forwarded to an externally visible, cloned version of your UX Style Framework with all the problematic fields removed. By doing this, you eliminate the need to maintain two separate sites (which will never work), while ensuring that important team members outside your firewall always have easy access the most current standards information.

HOW DO UX STYLE FRAMEWORKS EVOLVE AND CHANGE?

The key to having standards that grow and evolve over time is the implementation of a fast, simple, transparent change-management process which allows collaborative decisions.

© fotomaster / Fotolia

No matter how carefully researched, planned and documented they may be, your standards must evolve and change. Each time a popular website releases a new look and feel, or a new device is rolled out which introduces a new interaction, user expectations for your site or application will change. Some of these changes will be dramatic, some will be incremental—but changes are inevitable.

This is the area where many traditional style guides fall short. Because they are static by nature, there is no process built in to address the constant stream of incremental changes that simply must be incorporated for your standards to stay relevant. Many style guides try to address this problem by releasing updates with version numbers, but this often results in even more confusion. Users will simply grab the guide with the highest version number they can quickly locate—which may or may not contain the latest information.

UX Style Frameworks Embrace Change

By providing a single source for your standards, and providing the ability for everyone to add comments and ask questions, UX Style Frameworks provide a clean and transparent way to manage ongoing, incremental changes. In a future chapter, we will walk through common scenarios which result in a standard being changed. We will cover each step from the initial change request, through the exchange of comments and information, the decision making process, and how the change is then communicated to the company.

FIVE GUIDELINES FOR SUCCESS

In order to understand the true benefits of a UX Style Framework, we need to closely examine existing standards practices to identify the good, the bad, and the ugly. We'll carry forward the good—as there is much of it. But you must eliminate the bad and ugly, as they fuel ongoing conflicts and make document maintenance nearly impossible.

After reviewing countless standards, I've identified five guidelines to help ensure your framework's ongoing success:

- "There can be only one"
- "You only have five minutes"
- "Keep it simple"
- "Say what you mean"
- "Think republic, not dictatorship"

1   ## "There Can Be Only One."

Take a moment to consider the amount of standards documentation that currently exists within your organization. First, your engineering team has built component libraries of reusable code which they access regularly. These libraries save thousands of dollars in development time, as it is much faster to reuse previously-tested, existing code than to write from scratch. On the other side of the building, your marketing department has spent tremendous effort defining your company's brand, which is usually detailed in their brand or style guides. If you have a dedicated UX team, that group has created pattern and asset libraries to document effective interactions which have been validated by user testing and industry best practices. And finally, your designers (who are often spread across multiple teams and outside agencies), are using shared server space to store the templates and other visual artifacts needed to create their visuals, rapid prototypes, and final engineering assets.

When I began looking at all these documentation sources, I quickly realized that a huge amount of information was duplicated between them. For example, all of them contained definitions for fonts, colors, buttons, link behaviors, etc. The more detailed the documentation, the more similarities there were.

Based on this early research, I estimated that at least 80% the information documented by each group overlapped. While that 80% figure may surprise you, the truly important word in that sentence is "overlap." Notice that I did not use the terms "match" nor "duplicate," as it is the huge amount of *conflicting* information between these documents that is at the core of inconsistent standards problems.

This overlap is one of the reasons your company continues to have debates, email churn, countless revisions, ongoing change requests, and one-off solutions which require custom coding —the symptoms of conflict are nearly endless.

When I first presented this 80% number to my publisher, the technical editors (some of whom are very well known UX professionals) challenged that number. No one thought it could possibly be that high. So, I was asked by the publisher to supply research to verify my claim. As far as I know, no one has ever actually researched this topic, therefore I had to take it upon myself to validate the number.

THE METHODOLOGY I started my research by creating a list of the UI elements and interactions defined in the popular presentation layer coding framework, Twitter Bootstrap. Then, I gathered representative samples of online brand/style guides, UX pattern libraries and development code repositories. Some of these were internally published sources from my former or existing clients including Citi, Expedia, Travelocity, Bank of America, and AT&T. Others were corporate standards and user interface guidelines currently available to the public, such as Dell, Microsoft and Apple. I also included material from UI resources like Yahoo Pattern library, UI Patterns, and DesigningInterfaces.com.

I expanded the Bootstrap list with other elements and interaction patterns commonly appearing within all these additional sources. That brought the final count to 124 core elements, interactions and content formats. I placed these into a chart with three columns: one for marketing style guides; a second for UX pattern libraries; and a third for development code repositories.

For each design element, I placed a bright orange check mark in the corresponding column when an element was regularly included in that particular document type. I used a gray check mark if the element was included, but only partially defined. The full chart is shown in Appendix A.

THE RESULTS   Out of the 124 defined elements...

84 were documented in all three sources.
32 were documented in two of the three.
only **8** elements appeared in a single source.

93.5%
ACTUAL OVERLAP

So my 80% estimate was indeed inaccurate—but not in the way everyone expected.

This research uncovered another sobering statistic for executives: If 93% of elements are documented in all three sources, then your marketing, UX and development departments are re-creating one another's work over 66% of the time. While standards are indeed important, needlessly duplicating work is definitely *not* the most efficient use of such valuable human resources.

But let's look at the most critical problem created by all this duplicated work.
With a 93% overlap, what is the probability of there being no conflicting information?
I doubt I need to present additional research for you to agree that it is most likely 0%.

Logic dictates that whenever there is a conflict, at least one source must be wrong. However determining *which* set of standards is wrong seems to depend entirely upon which group you happen to be speaking with at the time. I recently gave a UX Style Framework presentation to an enterprise development team, and I was later told one of the engineers said, "I don't know what she was talking about—everyone knows the code repository *always* has the correct definition." Apparently "everyone" excluded the designers in the marketing department, who had no idea a code repository even existed, let alone any idea how to access it.

The Hard Truth: If people believe standards documentation is incorrect,
they will simply ignore it.

© Forgiss / Stockfresh

If the marketing team believes your existing site is not displaying their branded elements correctly, new visual designs will ignore all previously coded work—effectively negating the value of any reusable code library. Conversely, if your engineers are facing a tight deadline and see a conflict between their approved code repository and the visuals submitted by the design team, they will implement existing code to ensure the product launches on time.

Discovering that months of hard work is being routinely ignored by other groups within the company is not what anyone wants to hear, particularly after investing countless hours defining a style guide, building a pattern library, or testing code for a repository.

If your standards are documented in two or more places, there will inevitably be conflicts between those sources. As a result, you will have very few truly universal standards. So, let's rephrase Guideline #1 because it is so critically important:

To minimize conflicts and ensure your standards are enforceable across multiple groups,
a Style Framework consolidates these cross-departmental materials into a single location.
It provides an easily accessible, and easily understandable, one-stop reference
for every person, in every department, company-wide.

2   "You Only Have Five Minutes."

Remember the Waldo® books? If you are like me, you loved going through all the pages, racing against your friends to see which of you could find Waldo first. But imagine that same book on the last day of a sprint, with a project manager emailing you every 15 minutes asking, "Did you find Waldo yet? How much longer is this going to take? When can you start on the next page? Everyone is waiting. Did you find him yet?" Under those conditions, I don't think the Waldo books would be nearly as entertaining.

© mariae / BigStock

> If the person using your standards documentation cannot find the information they need in under five minutes, they will stop looking and create something visually similar from scratch.

People looking for information within standards documentation follow similar steps: First, they scan the table of contents or index, hoping to recognize a keyword. Next, they will flip through the pages, looking at section headings and pictures. A few may even read the first sentences of copy or examine a chart on pages of possible interest. But most of the time, a user's only real goal is to find the single piece of information needed at that particular moment. As a result, very few people will actually read anything more than the page headings.

Ironically, even the people who originally created your standards will rarely re-read the details. Otherwise, the documentation would not be loaded with typographical errors and inconsistencies—many of which testify to the creator's liberal use of "copy and paste."

© Tonic3

The binder shown above is an actual example of one company's assembled standards documentation. It contains over 500 pages of detailed information on everything necessary to create an online application; colors, fonts, margins, padding, positioning of elements, etc. Before this single binder was assembled, there were five separate sources of documentation—each one created by a different group. As covered in the previous chapter, users ran into conflicts between those various guides and decided to assemble everything into one binder, grouping like items together (buttons, navigation, form elements, etc). Doing so helped them locate items more quickly, and ensured conflicts could be identified and resolved.

But take a moment to put yourself in the shoes of a new UX designer at this corporation. Let's assume you have been asked to find the approved visual styling for a disabled button. Where would you even begin to locate that information in an un-indexed document this size? To make matters worse, this compiled source was only available in print, making it impossible to run an electronic search. But even if the five original sources were available in .pdf form, the term "disabled" might appear on 50 of the 500 pages.

Having watched designers and developers for years, I can tell you what many of them will do to solve this particular problem: They put the book aside, and go to the corporation's live site. They click around until they find an instance of a disabled button. They will then take a screenshot, open the image in their favorite graphics editor, and grab the correct color by using....

© yusak_p / BigStock

...THE DREADED EYEDROPPER: THE STARTER DRUG FOR KILLING STANDARDS.

While the eye dropper may seem small and harmless, it is not. You need to be aware that it is an early symptom of the eventual death of your standards. Regular use of the eyedropper by designers and developers means they are no longer accessing standards documentation—usually because they cannot quickly locate the information they need.

The eyedropper creates havoc because there is no guarantee the selected live-site sample is "known good." If there were no conflicts between departmental standards, and if there were no legacy pages, and if nothing was created by outside vendors, then perhaps "death by eyedropper" would not be so swift. But as your team becomes further detached from your standards, many other bad habits, such as using marquee boxes to guesstimate pixel measurements and positioning, will emerge. The more tech-savvy employees will begin using Firebug or Chrome Developer Tools to pull specifications from the published CSS.

If your team is heading down this path, in no time at all you'll have a site with disabled buttons that may appear virtually identical, but will actually use 58 different shades of gray and be 114 different sizes. At that point, you might as well put your CSS inline—the lack of consistency will eventually make every element on your site a one-off.

Your users must be able to find accurate definitions for elements in less than 5 minutes—with the emphasis on "less." UX Style Frameworks solve this problem by providing a logical hierarchy, relevant open text search capabilities, and large images. All of these work together so users can rapidly locate and identify needed information.

3 "Keep it Simple."

There is a great classic rock song by the band 38 Special that says, "Hold on loosely, but don't let go. If you cling too tightly, you're gonna lose control." Nothing could be more true, particularly when it comes to standards. Take a moment to examine this sample style guide page:

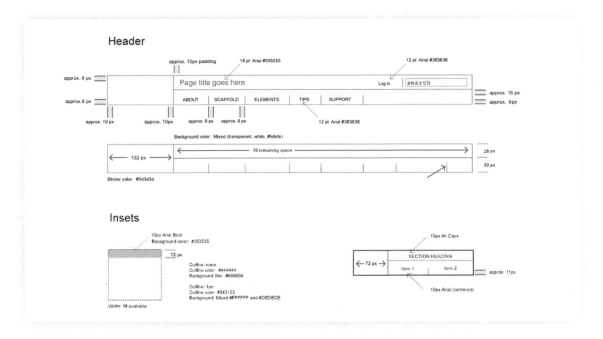

I will respectfully submit that this example does not present styles nor standards, but detailed visual design specifications. Worse, it uses ambiguous specifications such as "*approximately* 8 pixels."

This example showcases "Rules-Based Design" in its highest form. If your standards have pages which include this level of detail, be prepared for them to fail—just like Jared Spool said. I know, because most of my early style guide pages looked exactly like this.

The problem is that highly prescriptive specifications are inflexible and cannot grow nor evolve over time. While a heavily documented solution may work for the first round of pages created, problems will emerge when it is time to build the next round. More likely than not, there will be new business or user requirements that will force the designer or developer to break at least one of the rules shown. And once that first rule has been broken, it is relatively painless to break another… and then another…

Ironically, while designers complain endlessly about this type of prescriptive documentation, it exists because it gives the original design team a highly seductive illusion of control. In their minds, this level of detail is necessary to capture their vision perfectly and ensure pages will be constructed by developers exactly as they were designed, down to the pixel.

© Lightsource / Stockfresh

Therefore, it is not difficult to see how style guides can quickly devolve into detailed visual specifications. But business requirements and user needs are anything but static, and the specifications created for today's problems will be totally useless tomorrow. When creating your standards, you must push for simplification, and define only basic elements. This will give designers and developers the flexibility to combine elements to address specific needs without sacrificing consistency.

While detailed visual specifications are important when building a specific page, standards must be applicable to *many* pages and must evolve over time.

UX Style Frameworks address this by defining only basic elements and interactions. These are then freely combined into more complex widgets and pages, providing both consistency and flexibility to your site or application.

Although all UX professionals recognize the need for standards and consistency, they also know that it is impossible to simply "paint by numbers" if you want to build a truly effective website or application.

A quick story: In early 2010, I proposed an interaction for an e-commerce client which allowed users to rapidly scan sale items clicking a series of "flip cards." I was extremely confident in this solution, but as a matter of good practice we went to user testing. I was shocked to discover that customers did not like my proposed interaction at all. Rather than a flip interaction, they overwhelmingly preferred to see cards in a grid. As a result, a grid view was written into the standards as the preferred way to present multiple sale items.

However, during a second user test only six months later, the results were completely reversed. This time, users overwhelmingly preferred the "flip card" solution. What happened in the interim? Users had become familiar with the flip interaction through gaming consoles as well as popular sites such as Netflix. In only six months, this previously unfamiliar interaction had become common, and therefore acceptable and desirable. Had that company been unable to update their standards quickly to incorporate these new test results, their pages would have started to look "old fashioned" very quickly.

© HASLOO / Stockfresh

The blunt truth is that user interface design is a fashion industry. If UX and development teams are forced to retrofit all new components and pages into previously defined and accepted interactions and templates, the inevitable result will be an outdated, conventional, and potentially ineffective application. It may work, but it will not delight your users.

Each new device has the potential to redefine what customers consider "common." Unlike overly prescriptive style guides, a UX Style Framework will not shackle your teams, but provide options to create the best solution for each particular task. Plus, your standards will be able to quickly evolve and keep up with newly emerging interactions and styles.

"Say What You Mean"

As UX professionals, what we do for a living is very precise and our attention to detail is critical. In most programming languages, the omission of even a single semi-colon from a line of code can prevent an entire page from loading. Paradoxically, the words we use to describe the elements and interactions we build are often ambiguous at best. This can create a lot of drama when communicating with colleagues.

WHAT DO YOU CALL THIS INTERACTION?

For example, what do you call the common interaction shown below? The user clicks a link, and the page darkens. On top of the darkened page sits a container with content. The page below is basically disabled—the user must either interact with the container, or click somewhere to close the container in order to return to the page underneath.

Is this a modal? A lightbox? An overlay? A dialog box? A popover? A pop-up?

The truth is, this particular interaction has been called all those things. This isn't horrible in and of itself, but when one of those phrases, such as "dialog box" is also commonly used to describe a completely different interaction, miscommunication can happen very quickly.

Not long ago, I was told about a product manager who was very opinionated about the way her pages were designed. She kept insisting that one of the pages needed a dialog box in order to more fully explain the product. The Development team pushed back, stating that feature was unnecessary and that her request was overkill—but she would not give up. Realizing this particular debate might jeopardize the launch date if not settled soon, the developers gave in and coded the interaction they called a "dialog box." It looked like the top illustration.

© Bootstrap

The product manager saw this and exclaimed, "What on earth is that? I wanted a dialog box!"

The developers rolled their eyes and replied, "This *is* a dialog box."

She rolled her eyes right back and said, "No it isn't. *This* is an example of a dialog box." She then showed them the lower image: an interaction where rolling over an object caused a small container, resembling a cartoon speech bubble, to appear.

They replied, "That's not a dialog box. That's a tool-tip."

She said, "A what? Don't be ridiculous – everyone knows what a dialog box is."

This single misunderstanding resulted in nearly 200 unnecessary emails, 3 completely unproductive meetings, and 2 weeks of coding that ended up being thrown away.

Multiple documents will lead to multiple words — and inevitable conflicts or misunderstandings. UX Style Frameworks define a consistent vocabulary that is necessary to accurately describe designs/ideas to multiple groups.

"Think Republic, not Dictatorship"

If there is an individual within your company who...

© Fernando_Cortez / Stockfresh

- Knows the exact market positioning of every product you sell, and has access to detailed user research on every segment of your customer base

- Can explain your entire brand strategy and corporate vision from mass-market media down to simple emails

- Is intimately aware of the profitability of your individual product lines

- Stays up-to-date on cutting-edge usability best practices, research, and user testing methods

- Has award-winning experience designing interactions and visuals

- Is an expert on SEO, web analytics, and accessibility requirements

- Can write flawless HTML/CSS and Javascript to create fully responsive websites, as well as native code for mobile devices

...then perhaps that lone individual *might* be able to write and maintain your documentation. But for the rest of us, having a "Style Dictator" is another sure-fire way to kill standards.

Dictatorships always fail. If standards are defined by one person or one team, they will die. Could be a slow death, could be a coup d'état. But the end result will be the same.

Standards dictatorships are equally fatal whether controlled by an individual, a business unit, or a whole department. It is impossible for one person or team to have the full depth and breadth of knowledge necessary to ensure truly functional standards for online experiences. In addition, they filter all their decisions regarding what to include, omit, prioritize, and minimize based on their own group's assessment and knowledge of each item.

Consider these examples: Marketing departments are often surprised to learn their brand colors do not have sufficient contrast to be ADA compliant when used on a web site. Visual designers sometimes include large photographs without consideration of page weights and load times, particularly on mobile devices. Developers inadvertently stretch or distort logos and leave off registration or trademark symbols, then commit the code without realizing the page violates branding and perhaps even legal requirements.

While all of these issues have workarounds, it would be much easier if proposed standards could be discussed and vetted with *all* impacted groups. It is intriguing to note how many companies pride themselves on engaging cross-departmental teams, and even their customers, during the development of new products and services. Yet those same companies permit the standards which define their online user experiences to be defined in isolated silos.

To make matters worse, dictatorships aren't limited to the definition phase—if one person or department can override existing standards at will, they are basically exercising the same dictatorial powers.

> In the real world of standards documentation, there are often multiple dictatorships. Like the warring city-states of old who were often unwilling to compromise, each of your departments creates its own variation of the standards through its own filter. They each spend countless hours working and refining the included elements, researching best practices, and carefully preparing copy and supporting graphics. The final documents are distributed around the company, the conflicts between them are uncovered...
>
> ...and you end up going full circle back to the need for Success Guideline #1: "There can be only one."

While this chapter may have made you smile while reading passages describing your own experiences and observations, I also hope it gave you insight into many of the problems with existing standards documentation formats. These success guidelines should help you recognize the practices that work, as well as those that do not.

But whether you adopt a full UX Style Framework as it is described in upcoming chapters, or if you decide to simply modify your existing style guides to incorporate some of these techniques, adopting the success guidelines will help keep your standards alive.

A DAY IN
THE LIFE OF A
UX STYLE FRAMEWORK

In the previous section, I introduced the core concepts behind a UX Style Framework. I also shared a few guidelines which can help ensure the success of your standards. Next, we will take a closer look at the day-to-day processes for creating, using, and managing a UX Style Framework. How will it be used by people within your organization on a daily basis? Who makes the decisions on what to include? How are changes suggested? How are disputes settled? Who owns it?

And perhaps the question I am asked most often, "How can I secure the support within my organization to actually implement a UX Style Framework?"

OWNERSHIP

Previously, we discussed the differences between a UX Style Framework and traditional standards documentation. But the success guidelines state the framework cannot be owned nor controlled by one person or team. So who owns it? Who decides what to include? How are changes handled? How is it maintained? How does the decision making process work?

This chapter will focus on the ownership of your UX Style Framework. We will define the roles and responsibilities of its owners, their day-to-day tasks, best practices they can adopt when making decisions, and how they effectively communicate those decisions to the company. We will also review the ownership structure for the maintenance of the UX Style Framework itself.

OWNERSHIP ACROSS A DISTRIBUTED NETWORK

The platform and organization of a UX Style Framework ensures that the creation, maintenance, and ownership of your standards is controlled by a distributed network of people. This concept of shared work and accountability is based upon two highly effective tech industry models: The modern data center and open-source software projects.

© kubais / Stockfresh

The Benefits of a Distributed Network

From the earliest days of computing, it became clear that having everything centralized on one large, powerful computer was tremendously risky. If that system went offline, for any reason, everything stopped.

To minimize risk, modern data centers distribute processing across a large number of smaller computers. By doing so, no single box can become overloaded during peak demand times. Plus, if one unit should fail, the workload is split across the remaining systems within the network with no perceptible loss in performance. As a bonus, having multiple systems makes it much easier to run cross checks to identify errors and conflicts.

UX Style Frameworks are designed to work the same way. Even if we put aside the problems associated with design dictatorships, it is simply too much work for a single individual or group to be fully responsible for the ongoing, timely maintenance of a company's style guide.

Consider the effort put into the initial creation of your current standards documentation. If you work for a large corporation, it was no doubt a herculean task. From the viewpoint of your executive team, such efforts seem twice as expensive as they require valuable human resources to be diverted from doing billable work. However, most companies do understand the importance of standards, and management will normally approve the time needed for the development of a guide.

However, style guides do not fail because of the time required for their initial creation. It is the style guide's ongoing maintenance and communication issues which present obstacles that often cannot be overcome.

Even when a company dedicates the time and effort to create a style guide, the unwillingness or inability to commit to that guide's ongoing maintenance is what leads to its eventual downfall.

In management's eyes, billable projects and immediate customer needs will always take priority over "in-house" work—particularly when that in-house project is perceived as complete. It is, admittedly, hard to argue against such a rational and justifiable position. Therefore, even when a style guide is controlled by a single department with the ability to make unilateral decisions on its content and changes, there will be an ongoing struggle within that group to find resources with enough free time to make regular updates. When you consider additional complications such as working across multiple offices and time zones, it is not difficult to see how updates to style guides simply get pushed to the side—until the content within them becomes obsolete.

For all these reasons, it is imperative to implement a system which distributes the creation, control, and maintenance of your standards across many people and departments. Like a data center, distributed ownership and maintenance is the best and most efficient way to ensure your standards remain current and are embraced by your entire organization.

INDIVIDUAL PATTERN OWNERSHIP

In our data center model, the full workload is distributed across a cluster of computers. However, each individual computer within the cluster is assigned its own tasks, has a clear way to communicate with the network, and has built-in redundancy.

In a UX Style Framework, each standard has an owner.
These owners are responsible for all decisions, communications, documentation, and ongoing maintenance of their particular, assigned standard.
However, because the guidelines tell us "dictatorships never work",
no single owner can control the entire Framework—just ONE page.

When adopting a Style Framework, each pattern's owner becomes the undisputed, recognized subject matter expert for that particular standard within your organization.

- They make all the decisions regarding that pattern *without the need to secure approval from anyone else in the company.* (More to follow.)

- They do all the required research.

- They write the description and pattern specifications.

- They select and add supporting images, code samples, and links to assets or repositories.

- They perform and communicate all updates and changes.

- They address all posted questions or concerns about the standard.

- They provide links to usability tests and industry best practices to validate the standard's effectiveness.

- They can *choose* to escalate to management should any unresolvable problem involving the standard arise.

- They ensure any changes to the standard are communicated to everyone that may be impacted.

© Jagodka / BigStock

THE POWER OF THREE

Although a single UX Style Framework pattern can be comfortably supported by one owner, larger companies can improve overall quality and further minimize conflicts by adopting shared ownership. In this structure, each pattern is owned by representatives from three different departments.

- One from Business or Marketing;

- One from User Experience or Design;

- One from Development.

The Benefits of Three Owners

There are a number of good reasons to have multiple departments share the ownership for each standard. Consider the following:

1. Each owner can represent their department's requirements/needs.

Not only will each owner understand the critical needs and issues that impact their respective department, they can voice those concerns to the other owners. This will greatly improve the overall quality of your standards, as major requirements or restrictions cannot be overlooked. Having one owner from each group also eliminates the cries of, "this decision was made without our department's knowledge" and the costly rework associated with successful escalations.

2. A small group of three is manageable.

Three people can normally find the time to talk, work together, and actually complete tasks. Larger groups invariably become bogged down by processes and organization. In a large group, it is simply too easy for members to deflect decisions ("We can't decide this now because John is not here") and avoid individual accountability.

3. Small groups can actually resolve conflicts.

It will be impossible to develop standards that do not involve compromises. The visually stunning elements incorporated in print and television advertising as defined in marketing's brand guides are often coding and maintenance nightmares for the development teams charged with reproducing those visuals on the web. Such conflicts normally kick of a sequence of faceless meetings, with each department becoming increasingly entrenched in its position. The decision on what to adopt keeps being deferred until some poor executive (often with no real expertise on the topic being debated) is forced to make a call simply because time has run out.

Compare that scenario with the UX Style Framework process: Each of the owners know one another personally and respect each other's skills. They meet to review the problem, explain their positions, carefully consider options comparing the complexity of the coding versus the branding benefits. They may decide to create a rapid prototype and order a few quick user tests to gather data to support their recommendation. All of these steps lead to a rational, informed decision on the final standard.

While not perfect, a UX Style Framework's ownership system will resolve conflicts more efficiently, reduce hard feelings between various departments, and improve the overall quality and effectiveness of your site or application.

© michaklootwijk / Stockfresh

4. When an Owner leaves the company, their domain knowledge remains.

Inevitably, people will leave your company. Sadly, they often take a wealth of domain knowledge and subject matter expertise with them. Having multiple owners within your UX Style Framework minimizes that loss of expertise. During the process of creating and updating standards, each group of owners discusses and documents many opinions, topics and requirements. They learn from one another, and can transfer the knowledge to new owners as they are assigned.

OWNERS MUST HAVE AUTHORITY AND SUPPORT FROM MANAGEMENT

In order for a Style Framework to be truly effective, your executive team and management must acknowledge that each standard's owners have the *sole* authority to make final decisions regarding their assigned standard.

To put it bluntly: They must give up their right to "Management Override."

In defense of executives, most of your senior leadership will be perfectly fine with this concept. They are always busy and could honestly care less if your site's buttons are green or blue—so long as KPIs continue to improve. Objections to this particular concept are usually voiced by over-zealous middle managers who, for a variety of reasons, are not particularly comfortable with delegation.

However, if every proposed change to your standards must be reviewed each owner's respective manager, or escalated to an SVP before decisions can be made, your standards will be unable to evolve—and will become obsolete in short order.

In the next chapter titled "Getting Buy In," which provides information on effective ways to sell a UX Style Framework internally, I will cover a few additional methods you can use to address this particular problem.

© JanPietruszka / Stockfresh

TIPS TO FIND AND SELECT OWNERS
WITHIN YOUR ORGANIZATION

Once your UX Style Framework is published and employees see they have a true voice in defining the company's standards, you will probably not have a problem finding owners for all the various patterns. However, in order to get your UX Style Framework populated with enough information for a company wide roll-out, you must recruit at least a few volunteers from the beginning. So where should you look?

START WITH THE UX AND PRESENTATION LAYER CODING DEPARTMENTS...

Although business owners and marketing designers will have a great deal of influence on visual style, they do not normally encounter issues where the inability to locate or reuse an asset can result in missing a deadline. Therefore, your early pattern owners will often be from the two departments which have the most to gain from a UX Style Framework: the User Experience and Presentation Layer coding groups. These teams understand the need for evolving standards as well as the benefits of distributed workloads. As a result, they will have strongest desire to see the UX Style Framework project succeed.

NEXT, CONTACT BUSINESS OWNERS WITH "PET PEEVES"

Almost every business owner or product manager I've met during my career has at least one "pet peeve" user experience issue. These managers are usually quite easy to identify, as they tend to bring up their favorite topic at virtually every new UI review. These topics can include handling form errors, the visual treatment of disabled buttons, site-wide alert messages, or accessibility concerns. Simply offer these product manager the ability to "own" their Pet Peeve in the new framework, and they will likely jump at the chance.

IMPORTANT: Do *not* make an executive the owner of any standard.
Although the Senior VP of Development "technically" owns
all the coding standards for your organization,
that person will be *far* too busy to maintain this document.

Between these two groups, you will probably be able to find enough volunteers to assign at least one owner per pattern during the framework's early days. Let each volunteer select their favorite pattern whenever possible, but discourage them from signing up for too many. One owner per pattern will be sufficient to kick off your UX Style Framework, as you will be able to identify more owners as the project evolves.

In the next chapter, we will cover additional scenarios that may help you recruit owners in more change-averse or apathetic corporate cultures.

WHAT TO CONSIDER WHEN RECRUITING OWNERS

© leecisn / Fotolia

- First, look for personal interest. People are much more likely to become actively engaged when they can define, monitor, and defend standards they believe in. By matching owners with genuine interest, everyone will benefit from the owner's enthusiasm and knowledge.

- Next, look for subject matter expertise. Check with colleagues to find owners with past experience using or coding particular standards. Their experiences, both successful and failed, will provide invaluable insights.

- If you adopt a shared ownership structure, be sure to monitor the organizational rank of owners within the same pattern. Because the owners must have an equal voice at the table, it is not practical to assign a Director as the business owner and a junior developer as the coding representative. While the organization levels do not have to match exactly, try to limit the range to one-up and/or one-down.

- Don't allow junior people to sign up for critical nor controversial standards. There are any number of stable patterns that must be defined for consistency and will require regular updates. Allow enthusiastic junior people to participate by assigning them safe standards, regardless of their personal interests or passions.

THE FRAMEWORK OWNERS

Although the patterns within your UX Style Framework will be owned and defined by individual contributors throughout your organization, someone must own the structure and supervise the operation of the framework itself. I refer to this governing group as the "Framework Owners", although I have heard the term "Super Owners" used as well. This group can be best compared to the upstream developer committees common to open-source projects.

The Framework Owners should consist of no more than six people: Three VP or SVP-level executives from business, UX, and development respectively; and three mid-level, hands-on employees from within the same departments. All of these people should be passionate about supporting the UX Style Framework and be fully vested in its success. The executives will focus on promoting the visibility of the system and championing its benefits across the organization, while the three mid-level employees will have administrator privileges and be charged with the hands-on updates and maintenance of the framework.

KEY POINT: Although the Framework Owners own the structure and monitor the operation of the UX Style Framework, they do *not* control its content.

Framework Owners are responsible for...

- Assigning and removing owners from the various standards

- Setting up user accounts for employees needing login credentials.

- Developing all necessary training and documentation materials needed for both owners and employees to use the UX Style Framework effectively.

- Controlling the structure of all the pages and making any necessary updates required to keep the framework functioning.

- First-line support for the owners; answering questions and helping them with any problems that may arise.

- Reporting anyone abusing or compromising the system to that person's direct supervisor.

In addition to these tasks, the Framework Owners have one very specific responsibility that far exceeds corporate championship and maintenance. This additional role is the key to preventing the UX Style Framework from picking up the "bad habits" of its predecessors. That is...

> Whenever the owners of any standard determine that a decision cannot be made without escalation, those owners must escalate to the Framework Owners rather than their respective direct supervisors.

Because the Framework Owners are made up of representatives from business, UX and development, this group will have the business and technical expertise to objectively evaluate and debate the merits of any escalation. This variance from traditional corporate protocol is important for a number of reasons:

- Because three of the members are executives, this group will have the corporate authority to prevent others from randomly throwing "Management Override" cards—something which is both hazardous and demoralizing to any standards program.

- Because escalations go to this group rather than to the owner's direct supervisor, this process minimizes the ability of middle managers to influence decisions.

- In a shared ownership structure, this system gives the "odd man out" owner an avenue to be heard should they feel they are being repeatedly overridden by the other two.

- It gives the Framework Owners insight in order to make decisions on any teams' overall effectiveness, as well as determine when a particular owner should be switched or replaced.

© monkey_business / Stockfresh

While the Framework Owners are indeed responsible for the overall health of the UX Style Framework, it is important to re-emphasize that this group is spread across multiple departments, multiple corporate levels, and *they do not control the framework's content*. As a result, they cannot become style guide dictators.

This group will, however, need to have processes in place should one of its members leave the company. Some Framework Owners allow existing owners to nominate a colleague and vote, while others rely upon the C-level executive from the impacted department to assign a new representative. Whatever method is used, it should be spelled out in advance to eliminate confusion and hard feelings.

GETTING BUY-IN

Regardless of the benefits of implementing a UX Style Framework, no project can move forward without internal approvals and buy-in from key stakeholders.

As I'm sure you are aware, pushing true culture changes within an organization is a book in itself and we clearly do not have enough time here to review every scenario. However, I am happy to share some of the common objections and hurdles I have encountered when proposing UX Style Frameworks within various organizations. Hopefully, these will give you ideas to help sway the powers that be to approve this particular project.

KICK-OFF CHAMPIONS

First, you are going to need a UX Style Framework Kick-off Champion—hopefully more than one. Since you have taken the time to read this far, your Kick-off Champions will probably consist of yourself and a few other like-minded individuals who recognize the genuine benefits of this new approach.

As a Kick-off Champion, you will lead the charge to gather internal and management support. You will need to explain the benefits of a UX Style Framework, and fully understand how it differs from traditional style guides in order to respond to questions. You will also need to recruit the first group of owners to help with the initial launch. But change is never easy, and most people within your organization are strapped for time. Even those who recognize the immediate benefits of a UX Style Framework may seem reluctant to volunteer to actually make these changes happen.

© Ollyy / Shutterstock

This not because they fear additional work—more often it is because they fear additional work that may turn out to be meaningless. Many have seen previous style guides rolled out with great fanfare, only to see those efforts overridden at will and abandoned within months. They know their colleagues regularly ignore published standards—because they are guilty of doing the same thing.

Do not become discouraged. At first, many people may seem reluctant to dedicate the time. No matter how eloquently and passionately your Kick-off Champions state your case, in order to gather support for your cause, you are probably going to need more compelling recruiting tools than a simple slide presentation.

THERE'S NOTHING LIKE "THE REAL THING"

If your managers and prospective owners can actually see a working example of a UX Style Framework before they are asked for support, getting approvals may be much easier.

BUILD A "PROTOTYPE"

If you or someone on your team is familiar with the content management system WordPress, you can create a working prototype of your company's new UX Style Framework in just a few hours.

Simply visit this book's companion website, StyleFramework.com. There, you will be able to request instructions to install an exact replica our sample site onto one of your own servers. All you need is access to a clean WordPress installation and to follow the directions which will be emailed to you. Once the clone is installed, add your company's logo, update the theme's colors and fonts, and perhaps edit a couple of key standards pages.

Being able to present a working prototype which clearly showcases the features and benefits of a UX Style Framework can be extremely compelling. Showing a version displaying your company branding is even more powerful, and it may minimize many of the perceived risks associated with approving this project request.

Showing a prototype UX Style Framework—one that your executives, department heads and prospective owners can actually see and use, is far more powerful than a static presentation. It is also more likely to secure the approvals you need.

The best news is this "prototype" is potentially not a prototype at all, but the foundation of your final site. It is a full working version of an actual UX Style Framework that uses placeholder data. If you opt to stay with WordPress as your final platform, you can simply copy your prototype to its final destination and you are ready to begin.

STEAL MY PRESENTATION

If your company is like most others, you will also need a traditional slide-based presentation on this topic. We have that ready for you as well. If you visit StyleFramework.com, you'll be able to locate a link to the latest presentation on UX Style Frameworks on Slideshare.net.

All the key benefits of a UX Style Framework, including most of the points from this book, are covered in this presentation: The success guidelines, the 93% overlap, what content is included, etc. All you will need to do is customize the presentation for your particular company, then grab a projector and get on someone's agenda. If you have created a prototype before your meetings, remember to add screenshots and live links to your own UX Style Framework on the slides.

Between a slide presentation covering all the key benefits, and an actual working prototype displaying your logo and corporate colors, you now have tangible items that will actively engage others and encourage them to support the adoption of a UX Style Framework.

Screenshot of the presentation on Slideshare.net

FREQUENTLY HEARD OBJECTIONS AND RESPONSES

Whenever I present UX Style Frameworks, I am often asked about common objections and how they can be overcome. Here is a list of additional information that may help you.

"WE SPENT A FORTUNE ON THE LAST STYLE GUIDE.
THERE'S NO TIME, NOR REASON, TO MAKE ANOTHER ONE."

There are many layers of possible objections hidden within this one, so I'll try to address them individually.

If your department owns the current style guide and this objection is coming from management, a "covert ops" tactic might be your best bet. Create the prototype site and begin copying and pasting your existing style guide content into it. A word of caution here: Your current style guide may be very complex. It will be very tempting to keep everything and simply transfer all your standards into the prototype. This will not create a UX Style Framework—it will create a huge, yet still traditional, online style guide. Use this opportunity to begin ruthlessly editing your styles to remove all the overly prescriptive items.

If your department does not own the current style guide and this objection comes from another group, try pitching collaboration. Ask if they are willing to combine their standards with yours into a new online format. Once the other team sees they can indeed retain ownership of the standards they care about, combining the guides may be an easier sale than it first appears.

"DEVELOPMENT ALREADY HAS A CODE LIBRARY"

If your development department is the hurdle, your tactic should be to "talk like a developer." Discuss the benefits of a common vocabulary, reusable code, and decreased development time. Emphasize that a UX Style Framework links to their code repository but does not replace it. Also, because each standard has a development owner, that team can now be involved when elements are actually being designed—something most want quite badly. And finally, remind them that collaborative ownership will prevent "pesky designers" from creating crazy things that must be coded as time-consuming one-offs.

"WE CAN'T SHOW INFORMATION OUTSIDE THE FIREWALL."

Although outside vendors and partners will find it extremely helpful to access your standards, it is not mandatory. If you run into a situation where your IT team or legal group insists that a password-protected site is not enough security, that is okay. Even if your UX Style Framework lives behind the firewall and can only be accessed within your network, the benefits are still substantial. Just accept that restriction and move forward.

"SOME (OR ALL) OF THIS INFORMATION IS PROPRIETARY."

Technically, if the outside world can see your site, there is virtually nothing about your visual or coding standards that isn't completely public already. However, as explained earlier, there are two options to overcome the "proprietary" objection. First is to build and work on the framework behind the firewall, and write a script to push an external clone with the proprietary information removed. Or, simply keep the framework behind the firewall as described above.

"WE WILL NEVER SUPPORT AN OPEN SOURCE CMS."

UX Style Frameworks are not restricted to WordPress. They can be built in SharePoint, other proprietary CMS systems, or even created with custom code. If you must use one of these other systems, simply follow the success guidelines and copy as much of the content and formatting as you'd like from StyleFramework.com. And by all means, forward us the link to your finished product so we can all learn from it.

"I TRIED ALL THIS, BUT THEY STILL SAID NO."

If you run into a stone wall, there are still some things you can do. Begin by incorporating as many of the success guidelines as possible into your existing documentation. Perhaps you can begin by stripping overly prescriptive content, or try to implement a shared ownership system so your style guide can be updated regularly. While these steps won't solve everything, they will help.

Worst case scenario? Simply wait 12–18 months and then ask again. If Jared Spool is correct, you current style guide may be obsolete by then.

COMMON DAILY TASKS

Perhaps the best way to illustrate the benefits of a UX Style Framework is to walk through a few common daily tasks. Let's take a look at three common user stories that your employees will encounter if you implement a UX Style Framework:

- Locating a Standard

- Designing a New Page

- Updating or Changing a Standard

You may discover that when everyone sees the framework's ease of use and experiences the genuine transparency surrounding its change processes, they are far more likely to embrace standards in their daily work.

As I present these examples, if you would like to follow along using a live UX Style Framework, visit StyleFramework.com.

TASK 1: LOCATING A STANDARD

Users trying to locate a particular standard within a UX Style Framework can search three ways:

1 **SCANNING THUMBNAILS ON CATEGORY LANDING PAGES**

Each of the major categories in your UX Style Framework should have its own Category Landing page. This landing page allows users to quickly scan large thumbnail visuals of each pattern. This method is best when users know the general function of the standard they need, but are not sure what it is called.

2 **BROWSING USING DROP-DOWN NAVIGATION MENUS**

Depending on the number of standards defined in your framework, you have the option of displaying a direct link to each standard under its respective category name in your main navigation bar. This method is valuable when the user knows the name of the particular standard they need, as the drop down provides a one-click link from any page on the site directly to their desired location.

However, this option may become impractical if your UX Style Framework has a long list of standards under each category. A word of caution is in order here: If this drop down navigation list becomes so lengthy that usability is impacted, you should pause and evaluate if your standards are becoming too prescriptive. Remember, a UX Style Framework should define only the building blocks of your site, not how they are arranged.

3 **USING AN OPEN TEXT SEARCH FEATURE**

Perhaps the easiest way to locate a standard within your framework is to use an open text search feature. On StyleFramework.com, clicking the magnifying glass in the upper right exposes a text search box. The user enters the name of the desired standard, and hits the "enter" key. This feature becomes extremely valuable when the owners include alternative names in the "this pattern is also known as" section (which will be covered in an upcoming chapter), as it easily redirects users searching for a different name to the pattern they actually want.

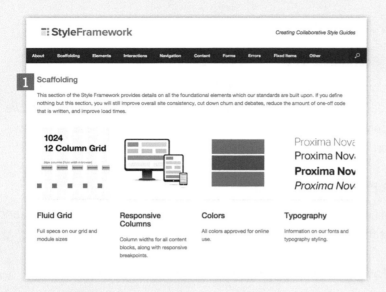

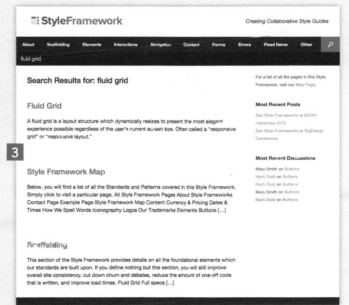

*Searching options within a
Style Framework*

TASK 2: DESIGNING A NEW PAGE

1 **Start with "Scaffolding"**

The foundational elements in a UX Style Framework are called "Scaffolding." These include items such as page dimensions, grid, typography and colors (we will cover Scaffolding in depth in Chapter 8). By starting with these, your new page will start to take shape almost immediately.

2 **Locate and Place the Appropriate Header and Footer**

Next, you will examine the business rules and locate the appropriate header and footer assets from within the UX Style Framework. Place them on your page.

3 **Copy and Paste All Other Necessary Elements as Placeholders**

Following your design sketches or wireframes, quickly rough-in the page by pasting containers, interactive templates, copy blocks and other requested placeholder elements from the UX Style Framework assets. This will allow you to quickly visualize the overall page and make spacing and item size adjustments.

4 **Replace Placeholder Text and Images with Relevant Content**

Once all the placeholder elements are on the page, replace obviously greeked items with more task-specific content and images. Normally this includes button and link text, headlines, and photography. Although the final copy and images may be revised later, your prototype will be more relevant to stakeholders and test subjects if you include content that is relevant to the page's purpose.

5 **Check Your Interactions and Present a Standards Compliant Page**

The final step? Load the page into a browser to ensure all your interactions and behaviors are working properly. Then present your fully standards compliant page for approvals and testing.

Not only is the initial creation of pages much faster when using a UX Style Framework, revisions or requests for multiple testing variations will also become streamlined. This is because all elements or components are built upon the same scaffolding.

1

2

3

4

5

TASK 3: UPDATING OR CHANGING A STANDARD

1 An Employee Submits a Comment or Suggests a Change

The first step toward updating a standard is for an employee to enter a request or suggestion into the comments area on the appropriate standards page. Anyone with access to your UX Style Framework should be able to enter comments. In the example shown on the facing page, Mary Smith, a visual designer in the marketing department, read an article on effective button shapes and wants to bring it to the attention of the button pattern owners.

2 The Primary Owner of the Pattern is Notified via Email

As soon as Mary's comment is posted, an email is sent to the primary pattern or standard owner (in the example at right, Marti Gold). The owner reads the comment and replies to Mary. *Important: this response is posted on the actual standards page and can be read by anyone.*

3 The Ongoing Exchange is Completely Transparent

From this point forward, when any comment is added, all current participants are notified via email. While a discussion is ongoing, anyone in the company may join simply by adding their own comment or question. It is very important that standards discussions take place in this type of open forum—no secret meetings nor "offline decisions" should be allowed.

3a

Side note: In many CMS/blog systems, the titles of all active discussions can be displayed in right-rails or dashboards so non-participants may join conversations of interest. On StyleFramework.com, we have a right-rail box titled, "Most Recent Discussions"—one click will take any interested user to the standard currently being discussed.

4 Decision to Update the Standard is Posted

Once it has been decided to change the standard (or to keep it as it is), the owners will post that information in the comment area. It often helpful if these posts use capitalization and/or follow a standardized format in order to visually stand out from other comments.

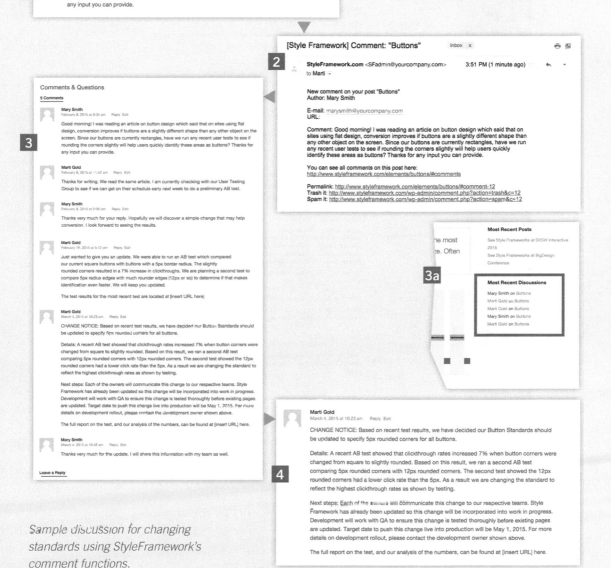

Sample discussion for changing standards using StyleFramework's comment functions.

Comment control screen within StyleFramework.com's WordPress administration area.

TASK 3A FOR OWNERS: MANAGING CHANGE DISCUSSIONS

During active discussions, the comment section can become quite long. All UX Style Framework owners should have "Editor" privileges within the system, allowing them to edit, delete, or archive comments on their pages. Here are some quick tips for owners to keep things under control:

1 **Reviewing Comments**

When an owner logs in, most CMS applications have some type of Dashboard area where new comments or notices are displayed. The owner will use this area to quickly scan for author, date submitted and page reference. It is a normally a good idea to set the comment display options so owners must approve comments by new users before they are posted. If that setting is enabled, comments awaiting feedback will be shown as "pending."

2 **Controlling Individual Comments**

The owners should have the option to approve/disapprove, delete, reply to, or edit any comment.

Move Redundant Comments or Questions into a FAQ response

During a discussion, owners may find a number of people are asking the same question or repeating the same opinion. Rather than deleting redundant comments to save space, consider making a new, single entry which paraphrases the question or opinion. If you do decide to combine multiple comments, be sure to include the names of the original posters to preserve the integrity of the discussion.

Ending a Discussion

Once a discussion has clearly come to a close, you may want to delete the comments in preparation for the next change suggestion. I recommend leaving the entry which contains the final decision in place so users can verify the date and outcome of the latest request. You may also want to archive all the comments into a single text file which can be added as a link if needed.

CREATING A UX STYLE FRAMEWORK

In previous sections, we have covered the benefits of a UX Style Framework, explained how it differs from traditional documentation, and touched upon its management and daily processes. Now we will go even deeper into the structure of the framework site itself. What are the different page templates? What types of content should be included on each page? How is the site organized and presented?

Although it is not required, feel free to follow along using our sample site, StyleFramework.com

GETTING STARTED

By this point, you have a solid grasp of the principles behind a successful UX Style Framework. Now its time to roll up your sleeves and get started with the creation of your own.

As we move forward, you will realize there is a great deal of flexibility when creating a UX Style Framework. But in order to effectively communicate how the framework should work, I will need to present some fairly specific examples. No doubt you will see different ways to organize your pages, or perhaps you will need to adopt different vocabulary terms. All of that is perfectly fine; you should feel free to adjust your UX Style Framework to fit your company's needs.

To satisfy minimum success guidelines, your UX Style Framework must meet each of the following criteria:

- Your standards should be presented in HTML/CSS, so they can be easily viewed by any web browser or mobile device.

- The site should be responsive, again ensuring its content can be accessed by desktop, tablet, or smartphone.

- Even the most non-technical employees must be able to use and understand it with virtually no training.

- The contents should be scannable, with clearly labeled images, so people can locate information quickly.

- It must have *accurate* open-text search capabilities, so those looking for precise terms can jump directly to a specific standard.

- All the content, as well as the site's structure and administration, must be controlled by non-programmers. Even the initial setup can require no more than minimal development support.

- It must allow anyone within the company to add comments or ask questions regarding any standard, and permit responses from the standard's owners.

- Ideally, it should be available outside your firewall so it can be accessed easily by external vendors and agencies.

And finally...

- All of this has to be extremely inexpensive. (Let me rephrase that – it has to be free. Because there is never a budget for internal projects such as this.)

© scyther5 / Stockfresh

I know what you are thinking.
"Seriously? Why not also ask
for World Peace?"
But I assure you that your new
UX Style Framework can indeed
meet all these criteria.

STEP 1: SELECTING A PLATFORM

Selecting a platform for my first Style Framework required extensive research due to the long list of factors to consider. I quickly realized that custom coding was not an option, as it required engineers and development resources (which seem to never be available, particularly for internal projects). Even if developers were available for the initial programming, a custom HTML solution would require the owners to go to development for even the smallest changes. That is not a viable solution for any document or website that needs regular updates in order to stay current.

With custom coding eliminated, I began looking into content management systems. Since budget was also a consideration, I knew it had to be an open source solution. So I focused on the most popular CMS options: WordPress, Joomla!, Drupal, and a Wiki.

The wiki solution lacked many of the customization features needed, plus editing within a wiki can often be daunting for novices. Jooomla! and Drupal were the most customizable, but that customization would have required development resources I knew to be unavailable at the time. Besides, since UX Style Frameworks are not particularly complex, those two seemed like overkill.

In the end, I settled on WordPress for the following reasons:

- It's free.

- It's powerful yet easy to customize.

- It can be set up and maintained by non-developers.

- Even the most non-technical staff members can use it with very little training.

- It has all the features necessary for a UX Style Framework to be viable—multiple user levels, comment sections, etc.

- There are literally thousands of plug-ins that can be added if the framework needs to be expanded.

I know what a fair number of developers are thinking right now: "Content Management Systems? WordPress? That's for novices. We are developers who write real code. So thank you very much for your suggestion, but we'll develop something internally that has the features we need and it will be much leaner."

It is true that you can create a custom solution that is leaner and will have all the features needed for the framework. But is that truly the best use of your development resources? Why reinvent the wheel when something as simple and reliable as WordPress or Drupal is available, particularly when they are both free?

Also, do you really want to internally support a custom site that is going to be in daily use by every non-technical person in your company? Once it is built, will you have the available resources to teach everyone how to use it? Will you have time to set up all the user accounts? Will there be someone available for desktop support and to answer emails and calls?

A CMS solution, while not as "sexy", will save you countless hours of grief compared to a custom code solution. Whether you use WordPress like our demo site, or whether you use another CMS of your choice, the pages and options necessary for a functional UX Style Framework do not stray from the default features of most popular content management systems. As a result, it's unlikely that there is any reason to re-create functionality which has already been written and tested.

WHY NOT SHAREPOINT?

I also looked at SharePoint as a platform, as it is widely used by corporations that could benefit from a UX Style Framework. Sadly, its feature set is greatly reduced for users not accessing it on a Windows machine; Plus, one of the benefits of a UX Style Framework is its ability to be shared with external vendors or agencies, and SharePoint sites are not usually accessible outside the corporate firewall. It may be a viable platform for this project if your corporation already uses it regularly; however, keep these caveats in mind before selecting it.

STEP 2: DEFINING THE HIGH LEVEL STRUCTURE

Once you have decided on a platform, lets take a look at some other structural considerations for a workable UX Style Framework.

Each standard should be on a single page.

In order for all the information supporting a particular standard to be easily located, everything must be in a single location. That means everything goes on one page. You must not give in to the temptation to split a standard up between multiple pages.

If you feel the page length and the amount of information for a particular standard is getting truly out of control and the amount of content is impacting the page's usability, remember: "Keep it simple." Confirm that all the information you are including is indeed relevant. Next, ask if the full information set needs to be included on the page, or if you can add a link to it.

If neither option reduces the weight of the page, opt for some sort of expand-collapse interaction to hide less critical data. One of those options will probably get the page length under control without requiring you to split the standard into two pages.

Put The Most Viewed Information at the Top; Least Viewed Toward the Bottom

While this may seem obvious, each department prioritizes information quite differently. In this instance, "most viewed" should apply to your end users. Every end user's first concern, when arriving on a page, is to rapidly identify the standard and answer the question, "Am I where I want to be?" Once that is confirmed, the user will scroll down the page to find the specific information they are looking for. Therefore, regardless of your final structure, insist that the top of each page display elements which focus on the identification of the standard rather than jumping straight into definitions or specifications.

Keep Section Subheadings Consistent from Page to Page

Next, pay attention to the consistency of your subheadings, both in wording and in sequence. Regardless of how your specific pages are organized, be sure to follow the same category/subheading order on every page. By doing so, users will quickly learn where certain data types are located on the page and be able to jump directly to the information they need. This consistency will dramatically decrease the learning curve of your framework.

4

No Section Should be Left Blank

If a particular section does not have any content, add a phrase such as "not applicable" or "currently under development" to the fields in that area. This ensures your users understand the area is intentionally left blank rather than assuming the page is incomplete. It is vital to remember that the UX Style Framework will become the single definitive source for the most current information on any standard. It is perfectly fine if information is missing or incomplete because a standard is still in the process of being defined, but be sure to let your users know about this.

© iqoncept / Stockfresh

STEP 3: CONTENT ORGANIZATION

Now lets look at the organization of the content within the UX Style Framework. With so many distinct elements, the information architecture of the site becomes critically important for users who need to locate standards quickly. Remember: "You only have five minutes." After a great deal of debating, user testing, and refinement of multiple frameworks, I have uncovered a few common patterns that you can adopt.

Top Level Content Categories

The most important navigation decision on most sites is determining top level content categories and their arrangement within the global navigation area. For my UX Style Frameworks, I have arranged the top level categories to move from left to right, going from the most foundational, simple items toward the more complex. Users will quickly recognize that core standards presented toward the left, such as the grid, colors, and containers are combined to create the more complex patterns defined on the right.

Top level categories for StyleFramework.com

We will be going to go into great detail about these categories, and the individual elements contained within each one, in an upcoming section. For now, the important takeaway is this...

Because simple standards combine to make more complex ones,
the UX Style Framework itself should be organized to emphasize
those dependencies and relationships.

STEP 4: TOP LEVEL CATEGORY LANDING PAGES

Once a user clicks one of the top categories in the global navigation bar, they should be taken to that category's top level landing page. As we've discussed previously, people trying to locate items in a hurry simply scan pages—they do not actually read. Therefore, for your UX Style Framework to be both effective and embraced by your users, keep the following in mind when creating category landing pages.

1 **Use Pictures as the Primary Identifier**

Because your users will be rapidly scanning the page, use pictures rather than words as the primary method for locating a standard or pattern. Using large thumbnail images will minimize the amount of time needed for users to identify the correct standard. Once located, the user can easily click down for full details.

2 **Support the Thumbnails with a Clear Name**

Associating the standard's name with its picture on the landing page will improve your user's confidence in his/her location. Just as important, this is your first opportunity to begin building a consistent vocabulary for various elements and interactions across the multiple departments within your company.

3 **Add a Brief Description**

Including a one or two line description under the standard's name will give additional information to the user in those instances where the static thumbnail and name may not clearly differentiate between similar patterns.

4 **Make Everything Clickable/Touchable**

All of the elements described here—pictures, titles and descriptions—should be interactive. Touching any of them should take the user to the respective standards detail page.

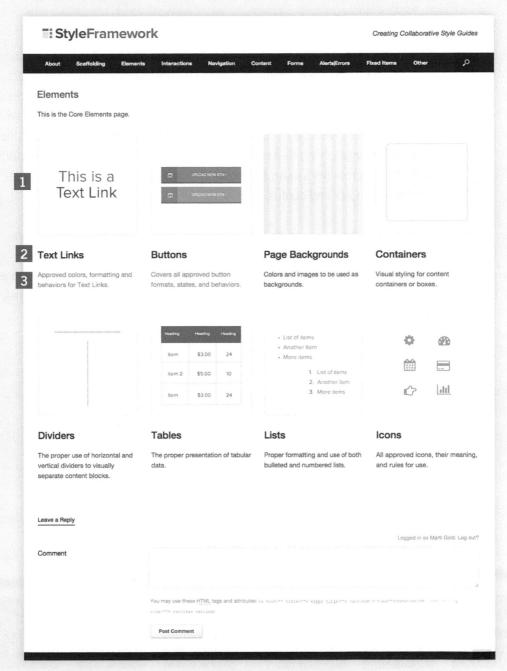

This is an example of a Category Landing Page on StyleFramework.com. Notice that each standard has a large thumbnail, a title, and a short text description.

Note: Don't be Afraid of "Pogo" Navigation

If your user does not see the standard they are looking for after scanning the landing page, they will normally go back to the top navigation bar and select another category. This can set up a navigation technique known as "pogo-ing" (drilling down, and then being forced to go up to a level in order to drill down into another section). While often considered a negative experience, don't be afraid of "pogo" navigation in this application. If you add super-navs, multiple fly-out menus, and cross-links in an attempt to minimize clicks, you may make the interface complex and confusing.

When designing your category landing pages, always remember the ease of locating information quickly is the most important consideration. Complex interfaces may do more harm than good. In this case, it's probably better to ask your user to click the main navigation bar or hit their back button than to risk getting lost.

Chart showing simple, high level navigation of the site.

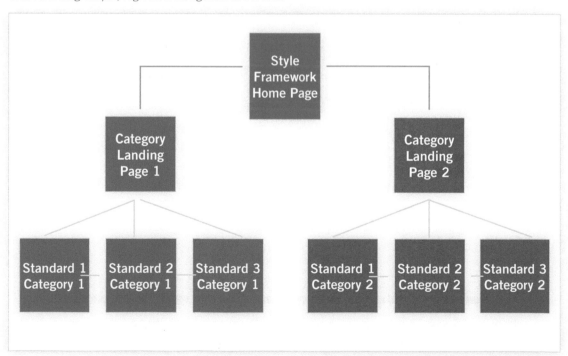

NAMING AND HOSTING YOUR UX STYLE FRAMEWORK

Because your Style Framework will be available online, it will need a URL. If that URL is difficult to remember, it could have a profound impact on the use of your standards. There are a number of options to consider when it comes to naming and hosting.

Option 1: A Stand-Alone Domain Name

Your first option is to secure a completely new domain name that is not affiliated with your company's primary domain. You can host this domain on either company-owned or external servers. A great example of this is Dell's pattern library, DellDesignLibrary.com. This option is an excellent idea if you plan to publish your standards externally and share learnings and best practices with the UX community at large. Conversely, unless the name is very simple and clear, it might be difficult for users to remember.

Option 2: Subdomains or Directories

This solution will tie your UX Style Framework URL to your company's domain name. Subdomains are usually formatted with the word "standards" replacing the more common "www" as in "standards.yourdomain.com." A top-level directory solution will have a URL that reads "www.yourdomain.com/standards." Either of these options will permit your standards to be visible outside your firewall, and are generally easy for users to remember.

On the downside, these names are controlled by company name servers and redirecting traffic will probably require some work from your system administration team. There is ongoing debate regarding which of these two solutions has more SEO value if that is important to you.

The important thing to remember is that regardless of the option you select, the URL for your UX Style Framework must be easy to remember. While users can indeed bookmark a framework site regardless of its URL, it is much better if they can hear the name once and remember it. This will ensure they can easily locate and access your standards from their home computer or mobile device.

PREPARING YOUR CMS INSTALLATION

Once you have determined a domain name and secured hosting, you will be able to install your selected CMS software. Most hosting services provide automatic scripts that can perform a basic CMS installation in as little as 3-4 minutes. If you are using company hosted servers, one of your system administrators will probably do this for you. Once installed, you will receive an administrator's name and password and can begin work on your own UX Style Framework.

Important Note: Because StyleFramework.com uses WordPress, the examples and instructions in this section have been written with WordPress in mind. For those of you not using WordPress, the rationale and goal behind each instruction has been included so you can make educated decisions on how best to use the platform you have selected.

INSTALLING A THEME

Many CMS platforms allow you to install themes to shortcut visual styling and functionality. My sample site, StyleFramework.com uses the free WordPress theme "Vantage" by SiteOrigin. Although StyleFramework.com uses the premium version, the free version includes all the functionality you need. I have also created Style Frameworks using the free theme, "Responsive." Both are easily accessible from the WordPress Dashboard.

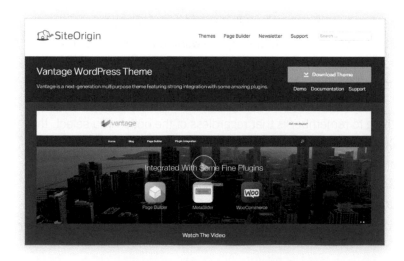

To see a live demo of the Wordpress theme "Vantage", which was used as the foundation for StyleFramework. com, visit www.siteorigin.com/vantage.

JUMP STARTING A UX STYLE FRAMEWORK

For those of you who may find it easier to edit an existing UX Style Framework rather than create your own from scratch, I have a solution that could save you a great deal of time.

Feel free to visit this book's companion website at http://www.StyleFramework.com and request instructions to create a clone of the complete StyleFramework.com site. This cloning process will place an exact mirror of StyleFramework.com onto your server, including all of its content, patterns, graphics, and even users. Please be aware that this process will overwrite anything you have previously created. However, if you are just beginning, this may be a great time-saving option to jump start your own work.

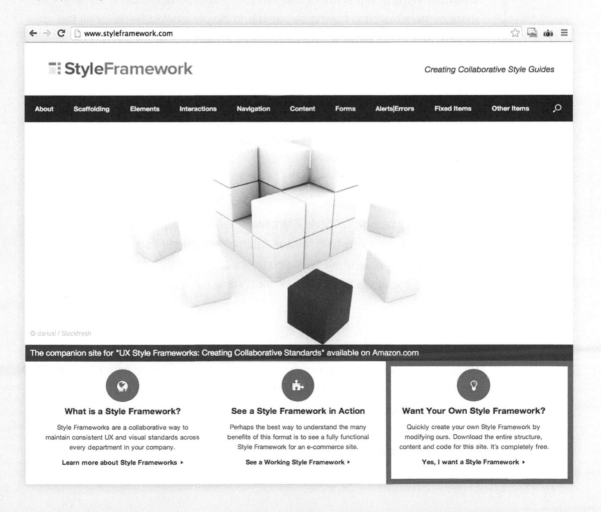

INSTALL ADDITIONAL PLUG-INS FOR ENHANCED FUNCTIONALITY

One of the beauties of an open-source content management system is the number of additional plug-ins you can install to make the creation and maintenance of a UX Style Framework much easier. While I will discuss specific WordPress plug-ins used on StyleFramework.com here, the important take-way is inclusion of the functionality described. If you use WordPress, all the plug-ins discussed here can be easily installed directly from the Wordpress Dashboard.

Advanced Custom Fields

Creates multiple content fields to help organize input.
Because many of your owners may have limited experience using content management systems, having separate and clearly labeled fields for all the individual content areas will make data entry much easier for them. This particular plug-in allows the Framework Owners to set up multiple content fields, customize labels, include instructions, set field types and character limits, and provide default or suggested content. While using a tool like this is not necessary, it will dramatically increase the likelihood that your standards will be updated regularly and minimize support requests from owners.

Akismet

Eliminates comment spam.
Because a successful UX Style Framework relies heavily upon comments, it is important to have a way to eliminate automated comment spam. This simple and widely used plug-in will save you hours of tedious comment deletion time, particularly if your UX Style Framework is living outside a firewall.

Child Theme Configurator

Protects your site's customization when a parent theme is updated.
Child themes permit you to make extensive customizations to your site that will not be overwritten should its parent theme be updated. From the author's site: "Child Theme Configurator is a plug-in to easily identify and override the exact CSS attributes you want to change, giving you unlimited control over your look and feel while leaving your Parent Theme untouched."

All (13) | Active (11) | Inactive (2) | Drop-ins (1)   Search Installed Plugins

Bulk Actions ⇕   Apply   13 items

	Plugin	Description
	Advanced Custom Fields Deactivate Edit	Customise WordPress with powerful, professional and intuitive fields Version 4.4.1	By Elliot Condon	View details
	Akismet Settings Deactivate Edit	Used by millions, Akismet is quite possibly the best way in the world to **protect your blog from comment and trackback spam**. It keeps your site protected from spam even while you sleep. To get started: 1) Click the "Activate" link to the left of this description, 2) Sign up for an Akismet API key, and 3) Go to your Akismet configuration page, and save your API key. Version 3.1.1	By Automattic	View details
	Child Theme Configurator Deactivate Edit Child Themes	Create a child theme that follows WP best practice to enqueue stylesheets. Easy to use CSS editor lets you find, preview and customize any style. Version 1.7.4.2	By Lilaea Media	View details
	Contact Form by BestWebSoft Settings Deactivate Edit	Plugin for Contact Form. Version 3.90	By BestWebSoft	View details	Settings	FAQ	Support
	Last Updated Shortcode Deactivate Edit	Creates a shortcode to display the date/time when a post/page was last updated (with optional formatting). Version 1.0.0	By bitacre	View details
	WordPress Twitter Bootstrap CSS Settings Deactivate Edit	Link Twitter Bootstrap CSS and Javascript files before all others regardless of your theme. Version 3.3.4-0	By iControlWP	View details
	WP Clone by WP Academy Deactivate Edit	Move or copy a WordPress site to another server or to another domain name, move to/from local server hosting, and backup sites. Version 2.1.8	By WP Academy	View details
	Plugin	Description

Bulk Actions ⇕   Apply   13 items

Thank you for creating with WordPress.   Get Version 4.2.1

*Additional functionality from WordPress
plug-ins used on StyleFramework.com*

Contact Form

Allows you to include simple contact forms.
This plug-in adds a standard contact form to your UX Style Framework. It is valuable for support questions unrelated to a particular standard that are directed to the Framework Owners.

Last Updated Shortcode

Displays the date of the most recent update to any standard.
If possible, you should find a way to display the last date and time a standard was updated. This allows users to visually confirm that the information being presented is timely and accurate.

Twitter Bootstrap CSS

Adds Twitter Bootstrap functionality to your Style Framework
This plug-in allows you to add fully functional Bootstrap components and interactions to your framework. This functionality is particularly useful if your development team uses Bootstrap on your production sites, as your framework can then precisely mimic many of the behaviors and interactions.

WP Clone by WP Academy

Create an exact clone of your UX Style Framework on another server.
Although it does not happen frequently, there may come a time when you need to make an exact clone of your UX Style Framework. In those instances, this functionality is invaluable. In one simple step, it permits you to make a exact mirror of any WordPress site, and then restore that site in another location. And by exact mirror, I do mean exact—structure, plugins, content, users, images, custom CSS—everything. Therefore, it must be used with some caution, as it will overwrite any existing WordPress installation at the destination URL.

WP Clone is the tool that will permit you to install an exact copy of our Style Framework on your own servers so you can begin customizing it right away. See page 75 for details on cloning StyleFramework.com

WHAT'S ON EACH PAGE

In order to help users locate information as quickly as possible, each page within a UX Style Framework should follow the same basic structure. In this section, we will be taking a closer look at the UX Style Framework page templates.

There are two main page types: the Category Landing Page template and the Individual Element Page template. First, we will examine the content on each page as it will be presented in the browser to your end users, explaining what information is included and why. Then, we will examine the corresponding area from within an owner's administration panel, where owners will work with the content and keep it current. The administration pages will discuss how and what to include, as well as provide tips for supplemental content to make your UX Style Framework even more useful.

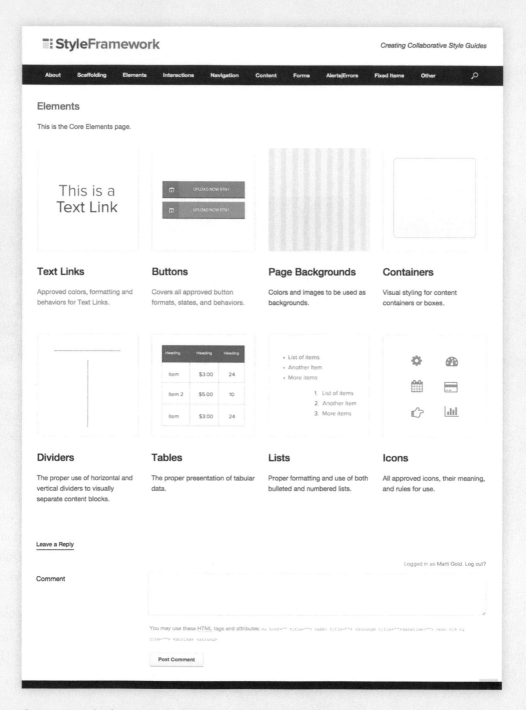

Screen shot of a Category Landing Page on StyleFramework.com.

CATEGORY LANDING PAGES

The success guidelines state "You Only Have Five Minutes" for your users to locate the standard or pattern they need, and we all know that users rarely read. As we learned in the previous chapter, each of the Category Landing Pages emphasizes large thumbnail images so users can visually scan the page and quickly identify what they need. Styleframework.com uses a square tile format that is both scalable and responsive.

In a Style Framework, Category Landing Pages are designed for quick scanning and identification of a standard. Therefore, they include only a large thumbnail, the standard name, and a 2-3 line description.

Category Landing Pages also serve as a visual "sanity check" on the level of detail within each section of your UX Style Framework. If the Category Landing Page grows past five or six rows, or 20-24 items, it is likely your framework is starting to become too detailed or prescriptive.

An increasingly large Category Landing Page is a excellent signal to the Framework Owners that it is time to work with the individual teams to re-evaluate the content within that section. They may decide to combine items, move them to a more appropriate section, or delete them entirely. But the key to any UX Style Framework is to include only necessary information and nothing more.

NOTE: To help you quickly differentiate between diagrams for pages displayed to end users and those showcasing owner administration pages, I will be using different colors for call-out numbers: **ORANGE** for display pages, and **BLUE** for administration pages.

ADDING OR EDITING CONTENT ON A CATEGORY LANDING PAGE

A first look at an owner's "Edit Page" administration area

As previously mentioned, StyleFramework.com uses WordPress as its platform, so some of the information presented here is specific to WordPress. If you are using a different CMS, it will still have an administration area or dashboard where changes and edits can be made, for instance the site's theme or design.

Depending upon the CMS and theme you select, many theme templates are built upon frameworks of their own. The "Vantage" theme selected for StyleFramework.com is based on a WordPress framework called Page Builder. Although it is not necessary to use the Page Builder tools to create and edit your Category Landing pages, their drag-and-drop widgets certainly make it easier to do so. *If you have cloned StyleFramework.com, this valuable and time-saving plug-in will be installed and activated for you automatically.*

After logging in to edit a Category Landing page, your owners will see the optional Page Builder interface shown opposite rather than a standard WordPress content box. Rolling over any widget will display its editing options.

1   The topmost widget holds the standard text description for the category.

2   The "tile" widget just below the text description is where owners will insert each standard's thumbnail image, name, and brief description. This area also permits owners to add the corresponding detail page URL, so that clicking the photo or descriptive text immediately takes the user to the desired page.

3   WordPress pages automatically present a revision history for the page just below the content area. This makes it simple to monitor when the page was last updated and who made the changes.

4   If your owner/editors know a few basic commands in HTML, it is not necessary to use Page Builder's tools. Simply clicking the button which says "Switch to Editor" will redraw the page and present the WordPress content box.

Screen shot of StyleFramework.com's "Edit Page" area within WordPress for a Category Landing Page.

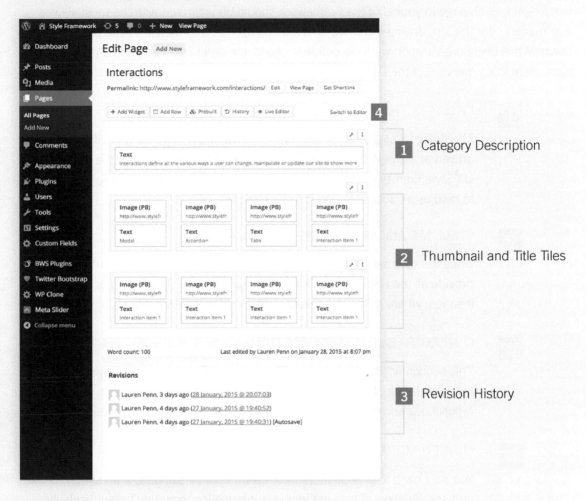

1 Category Description

2 Thumbnail and Title Tiles

3 Revision History

While this page may look somewhat daunting at first, please remember that once your standards are actually created, you will rarely need to make changes to a Category Landing Page.

THE DETAIL PAGE AND ITS CONTENT SECTIONS

Once again, each page in your UX Style Framework should be organized with the most viewed information near the top, drilling into more detailed and specific information as the page goes down. While every organization will have different needs, the order listed below is a good place to start. Here is an overview of the Detail Pages' sections, and what should be included in each one.

1 **"WHAT IS THIS?" SECTION**

The first goal of any layout is to help the reader quickly determine if they have arrived at the correct location. Therefore, elements displayed at the top of each UX Style Framework page should be focused on visually scannable information to help users accurately identify the standard.

2 **"TELL ME ALL ABOUT THIS" SECTION**

Once the user determines they are viewing the correct standard, this section will provide all the necessary details about that standard. This includes the problem it solves, where it should be used, and complete specifications.

3 **"I NEED TO BUILD THIS" SECTION**

This section will be accessed mostly by designers and engineers who need to incorporate this standard into their work. It will provide links to shared drives, repositories and code libraries containing production assets.

4 **"I NEED MORE DETAILS" SECTION**

You may need to provide more information about a standard than simply its use and specifications. This area includes information regarding recent usability tests, user research and other best practices.

5 **"I WANT TO CHANGE THIS" SECTION**

The heart of any UX Style Framework is the opportunity to propose changes to any standard, by anyone, in any department. The final section provides not only the contact information for the owners, but an open comment forum. Comments and questions in this section will be visible to everyone, ensuring transparent discussions regarding any decision impacting this particular standard.

"WHAT IS THIS?"

"TELL ME ALL ABOUT THIS"

"I NEED TO BUILD THIS"

"I NEED MORE DETAILS"

"I WANT TO CHANGE THIS"

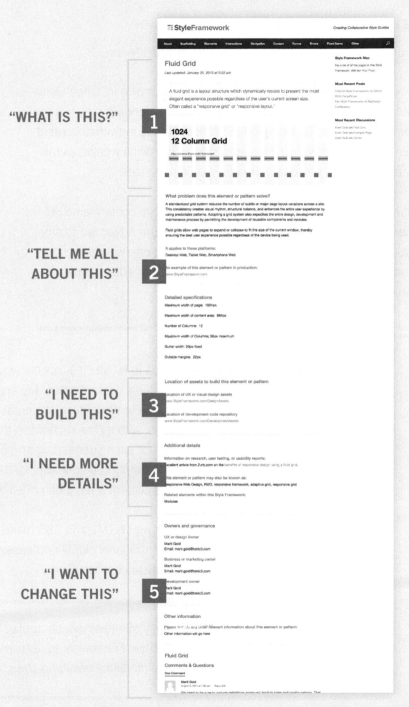

To see this page online, visit StyleFramework.com

ADDING OR EDITING THE CONTENT ON A DETAIL PAGE

The owner's corresponding "Edit Page" area within WordPress

If you have cloned StyleFramework.com, or have set up your own instance using Advanced Custom Fields, when your owners login to edit a standard they will see a screen similar to the one on the facing page. Notice that the individual content fields are presented in *precisely* the same sequence as the display page, as this will assist owners in locating the correct area for making changes.

Unlike a standard WordPress installation, which has one large content area or the Page Builder interface which utilizes widgets, we used the Advanced Custom Fields plug-in to create multiple content editing areas, each one with its own label and instructions. This makes the process of entering and editing data much less intimidating for non-technical users.

If your owners know a few basic commands in HTML, it is *not* necessary to use Advanced Custom Fields to set up multiple content areas. My first Style Framework used only the single content area in WordPress. We created a templated block of placeholder HTML code, with all the sections in the correct order, along with the necessary formatting for each subheading and content block. When a new page was needed, one simply copied and pasted the placeholder HTML block into the pattern's content area, then edited the text.

However, even those who are very familiar with HTML and CSS make mistakes. You may find they also appreciate the organizational clarity and ease of use associated with having separate, clearly labeled content fields.

The guidelines state, "You Only Have Five Minutes," which applies to editing standards as well. If you want your UX Style Framework to remain fresh, do everything possible to make ongoing maintenance easy and straightforward.

Screen shot of StyleFramework.com's "Edit Page" screen in the WordPress administration area.

SEC 1 "What is This?"

The first elements displayed on any UX Style Framework page should show the three main pieces of "scannable" information necessary for end users to visually confirm, "Yes, this is what I want." These elements should appear within the top 800 pixels of the page to reduce the need for scrolling. These items include:

1 **The Name of the Element or Pattern**

The element or pattern's name should precisely match the name that was used on the category landing page. This is important to reinforce a common vocabulary across the organization.

1a **The Date Last Updated**

While not critical, it is good idea to include the date when this content was last updated. Recent dates will increase your user's confidence in the validity and currency of the information on the page.

2 **A Brief Description**

A brief description provides a basic definition of the standard, element or interaction. For users, this is vital for clarifying the nature and purpose of the standard; for owners, the 4 to 5 line copy limit makes it impossible for highly complex interactions to become standards. This area should be visually differentiated using techniques such as larger type, wider line spacing, or perhaps a box in order to be easily scannable.

If an element or interaction is so complex that its brief description exceeds 2-3 sentences, it probably needs to be broken into smaller elements. An excellent guideline for is, "If you can't tweet it, reconsider it."

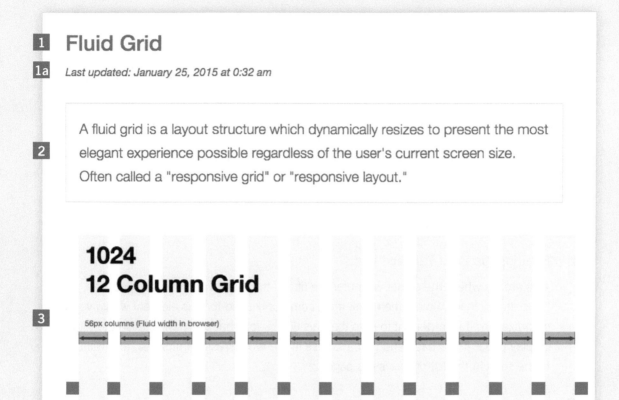

1 # Fluid Grid

1a *Last updated: January 25, 2015 at 0:32 am*

2 A fluid grid is a layout structure which dynamically resizes to present the most elegant experience possible regardless of the user's current screen size. Often called a "responsive grid" or "responsive layout."

1024
12 Column Grid

3 56px columns (Fluid width in browser)

Screen shot of a "What is This?" section on StyleFramework.com

3 **A picture or working example**

Unlike the visual thumbnail on the category landing page, the detail page should always include a large, clear image or picture of the standard. This is probably the most important area of the page, as the primary goal of this section is to help the user recognize the standard or pattern as quickly as possible.

CREATING OR EDITING THE "WHAT IS THIS" SECTION IN WORDPRESS

In WordPress, page editing takes place within the "Edit Page" section of the admin area. Thanks to the Advanced Content Fields plugin, each content area on the user-facing page has a corresponding field here, presented in the same order for quick association and easier editing.

Reminder: To help quickly differentiate between diagrams for display pages and those showcasing WordPress administration pages, I will be using different colors for call-out numbers: Orange for display pages, and blue for administration areas.

1 **Entering the Page Title and URL**

This area is where the owner will enter the title of the page, which should describe the pattern clearly. Select the name most commonly used for this element within your organization. It is important to note that this title is not what users will see on the top of the display page. It is a back-end name for use in the WordPress admin area, and will be the name seen in the list of your site's pages.

2 **Entering the Element or Pattern Name**

This is where you will enter the name of the element or pattern as it will be shown to end users. This name should precisely match the name used on the category landing page.

3 **Writing the Brief Description**

Use this area to enter a brief description for the standard. This description should be no more than 2-3 lines long. Although I did not place a character limit on this field on the StyleFramework.com template, you may want to do so. It is a required field.

4 **Adding an Image of the Element or Pattern**

If you used Advanced Custom Fields, this area will be set as an image field. It presents controls allowing the editor to select images from the Media Library, or upload an entirely new image. If you have opted to use a single content area, you can use WordPress's standard media upload functionality to add images.

Close up of the "Edit Page" screen showing relevant fields for this discussion.

SEC 2   "Tell Me More About This"

After the user has determined they are on the correct page by using the descriptions and visual cues in the "What is This?" section, they will continue down the page to gather more details about this particular standard. The "Tell Me More" section is where these details will be presented—what problem the standard solves, when and where it should be used, and where it can be seen in action. This section also includes the detailed specifications regarding the element's construction and interaction logic. Starting from the top of the section, your users will see the following:

1   What problem does this element or pattern solve?

While this question may seem self-evident, it is important to clarify the precise problem a particular standard is meant to solve. This tells user when the pattern should be used, as well as when it should be avoided.

For example, many end users confuse the functions "filtering" and "sorting." As many of you know, filtering results will reduce the number of items in any found set. Sorting does not reduce the number of items—it simply rearranges the existing set into a different order. However, your interface may need to give users the ability to filter (i.e. eliminate items outside a specific price range) and also sort (i.e. arrange the results to show lowest price first.). Because it is possible to both filter and sort by the same criteria, users frequently confuse these two.

Do not assume your users understand the purpose of the elements and standards included in the Style Framework, nor that they will immediately recognize when one standard should be selected over another. Clearly stating the purpose and function of every element is important.

1 ## What problem does this element or pattern solve?

A standardized grid system reduces the number of subtle or major page layout variations across a site. This consistency creates visual rhythm, structural balance, and enhances the entire user experience by using predictable patterns. Adopting a grid system also expedites the entire design, development and maintenance process by permitting the development of reusable components and modules.

Fluid grids allow web pages to expand or collapse to fit the size of the current window, thereby ensuring the best user experience possible regardless of the device being used.

2 ### It applies to these platforms:

Desktop Web, Tablet Web, Smartphone Web

3 ### An example of this element or pattern in production:

www.StyleFramework.com

4 ## Detailed specifications

Maximum width of page: 1024px

Maximum width of content area: 984px

Number of Columns: 12

Maximum width of Columns; 56px maximum

Gutter width: 20px fixed

Outside margins: 22px

Screen shot of Section 2 from the Fluid Grid page on StyleFramework.com

2 **It Applies to These Platforms**

Some elements or patterns are only applicable to specific platforms. For example, the fonts a company uses for its web sites may be different than those it uses in its compiled mobile or desktop applications. In those instances, the UX Style Framework may need to include two pages for typography— one for sites viewed in a browser, and another for standalone applications.

3 **Link to an Example of the Pattern on a Live Site**

It is always advisable to provide a link showing the standard actually being used on your live site. Presenting the element in context will normally clarify any ambiguity regarding its purpose.

4 **Detailed Specifications**

This area contains the information that many people consider the primary purpose of any UX Style Framework: the detailed specifications for a particular standard. Depending on context, this information could include sizes, interactions, colors, fonts, spacing, states, or any other details necessary to fully define the standard. It should also include information on business, legal, or regulatory restrictions that impact the standard.

This particular section can vary greatly in length from page to page, as some elements will need only a few lines of copy, while other may include charts, images, and even clickable samples (i.e. "click here to see an example lightbox").

By the time your users reach end end of the "Tell Me More" section, they should fully understand the standard and have all the information necessary to rebuild it.

CREATING OR EDITING THE "TELL ME MORE" SECTION IN WORDPRESS

1 **Writing "What Problem Does This Solve?"**

Editors of style guides often find this aspect of a pattern's description very difficult to write. In it, you need to clearly communicate the pain point this particular element or standard addresses. Because the purpose of many interactions, such as buttons, seem extremely obvious, they are often difficult to put into words.

However, it is important that you do so, as a clear definition of the solution will help your users objectively compare similar standards and chose the most appropriate one for their needs. If you consider the number of standards that provide similar functionality (for example, tabbed panels and accordions are both used to show and hide content), clearly defining which pattern should be used in a particular instance is critical for maintaining a consistent user experience.

Applies to Which Platforms?
This element or pattern may only apply to certain platform

- ✓ Desktop Web
- ✓ Tablet Web
- ✓ Smartphone Web
- ☐ Desktop App
- ☐ Tablet App
- ☐ Smartphone App

2 **Checking Platform Selection Boxes**

If you've used Advanced Custom Fields, this section will be set up as check boxes. Simply check all the platforms to which this element or pattern applies. The options will show as a line of text on the display page. This allows for the use of the search tool to easily locate all the standards which apply to a specific platform.

3 **Entering Links to the Live Site**

Regardless of the level of detail provided, sometimes the easiest way to demonstrate an element or pattern is to show it in action. If possible, set up this area as a WYSIWYG editing box, allowing owners to enter links that will launch pages utilizing this particular element. It is a good idea to include additional descriptive information when appropriate.

1   **What Problem Does This Solve?**

A standardized grid system reduces the number of subtle or major page layout variations across a site. This consistency creates visual rhythm, structural balance, and enhances the entire user experience by using predictable patterns. Adopting a grid system also expedites the entire design, development and maintenance process by permitting the development of reusable components and modules.

Fluid grids allow web pages to expand or collapse to fit the size of the current window, thereby ensuring the best user experience possible regardless of the device being used.

2   **Applies to Which Platforms?**

This element or pattern may only apply to certain platforms. Check all that apply

- ☑ Desktop Web
- ☑ Tablet Web
- ☑ Smartphone Web
- ☐ Desktop App
- ☐ Tablet App
- ☐ Smartphone App

3   **Link to our Live Site**

Provide a link to the live site where the element or pattern is used.

> 📷 Add Media

| B | *I* | ᴬᴮᶜ | ☰ | ☰ | ❝ | — | ☰ | ☰ | ☰ | 🔗 | 🔗 | ▦ | ✕ | ⌨ |

www.StyleFramework.com

p

4   **Detailed Specifications**

You may use this Wysiwyg editing area to add text, HTML code, or other formatting to provide full detailed specifications.

> 📷 Add Media

| B | *I* | ᴬᴮᶜ | ☰ | ☰ | ❝ | — | ☰ | ☰ | ☰ | 🔗 | 🔗 | ▦ | ✕ | ⌨ |

Maximum width of page: 1024px

Maximum width of content area: 984px

Number of Columns: 12

Maximum width of Columns; 56px maximum

Gutter width: 20px fixed

Outside margins: 22px

p

Close up of the "Edit Page" screen showing relevant fields for this discussion.

Entering Detailed Specifications

Of all the content fields within the Style Framework, this one has the most flexibility and will have the most variation in final size. Depending on the standard being documented, you may have to enter text specifications, tables, clickable examples, images, or any other type of information to help fully define the standard. In order to provide this flexibility, this field should be configured as a WYSIWYG editor, allowing you to enter everything from simple text to actual HTML code snippets.

Note: You may find it practical to replicate some information from other standards into this area (for example, including hex colors for text links that are also defined in the color section), but use your best judgment and keep your user in mind. While you don't want to unnecessarily replicate data (keep in mind that if colors are ever updated, you will need to go back and update any standard using colors as well), you also do not want to make the user run all over the framework trying to piece together information that could easily be compiled in this single area.

If appropriate, you can include business use cases or exclusions here. In general, it is better to over-document details in this section and edit later, rather than under-document and leave out important specifications.

If your technical skills are strong enough, you should consider adding actual code to create a working or clickable version within this section to supplement the static image shown at the top of the page For example, if you are describing the specifications for a modal or lightbox, what better way than to actually include a link or button which says "Click here to see a modal," and then trigger that particular interaction? This is particularly easy if you've added Twitter Bootstrap functionality to your site. By inserting the appropriate Bootstrap shortcode, you can easily trigger various interactions.

SEC 3 "I Need to Build This"

After a user has identified the pattern and learned more about it, they will reach the "I Need to Build This" section. This content is targeted at hands-on designers, UX professionals, technical analysts, and presentation layer developers. While the detailed specifications contain all the information to build a standard, this section gives those professionals time-saving links to the shared directories and code repositories containing the assets needed to create or fully document this particular element.

THIS SECTION ADDRESSES GUIDELINE #1: "THERE CAN BE ONLY ONE."

© dny3d / Stockfresh

Clearly all the different roles charged with building a web site or application need different assets. For example: Information architects will need templated wireframe assets; UX designers will need Creative Suite files; Technical Analysts will need Use Case or User Story templates; and Developers will need to access pretested code repositories. That said, it is impractical to assemble all those individual files, which are currently spread across multiple servers and supported by many departments, into a single location.

This is where the UX Style Framework shines. Simply by including links to all these important files on a single page, everyone involved in the creation of the standard can find the assets they need with just one click.

Location of assets to build this element or pattern

1 Location of UX or visual design assets

www.StyleFramework.com/DesignAssets

2 Location of development code repository

www.StyleFramework.com/DevelopmentAssets

Screen shot from the "I have to build this" section on StyleFramework.com.

1 Location of UX and Visual Design Assets

In order to construct a standard, the UX and design teams may need links to wireframe components, templates, color swatch libraries, or other files. By using this area, each of those teams can add a description of the asset along with a link to its location, so others can find it quickly.

2 Location of Development Assets

Links to code assets should allow the presentation layer developer to easily locate any HTML, CSS, Javascript or other production-ready code for that particular standard within your development code repository.

If your company has regulatory issues or internal processes which require complete written documentation for everything that is built, you may also want to include links to pre-written copy describing the standard which can be pasted and edited in Use Cases or User stories. Depending on your organization, these links can be placed in either the UX or Development area. Or, if these are very important, you may want to create a third content area in your framework called "Location of Technical Documentation Templates"

CREATING OR EDITING THE "I NEED TO BUILD THIS" SECTION IN WORDPRESS

Remember the 93.5% overlap discussed earlier in the book? When you begin consolidating all your asset links onto a single UX Style Framework page, those conflicts will be uncovered. While the volume may seem daunting at first, this single exercise is one of the most important steps you can take to get your standards under control.

1 **Entering the Description and Location of UX or Visual Design Assets**

When entering content for UX and visual assets, you can organize the content either by workflow or by department. Either seems to work fine so long as your description of the asset is clear and the location link works. Try to include the location of everything a UX designer may need, even if it is as simple as stating, "Hex colors used are defined on the 'colors' page of this framework."

2 **Entering the Description and Location of Development Assets**

Links to code assets should allow the presentation layer developer to easily locate any HTML, CSS, Javascript, or other production-ready code for that particular standard within your Development Code Repository or external framework library. If the code is behind your firewall, you may want to make a note that it is inaccessible outside the network and/or will require login credentials.

For Both Fields

When you run across conflicting assets (and you will), you have two options:

- Stop and talk to the different creators and try to get agreement on one or the other; or

- Enter both, state the conflict and the source of each one, and make a note that this issue must be resolved.

Which one you choose will depend upon your deadlines, the size of your organization, and the politics required to reach a consensus.

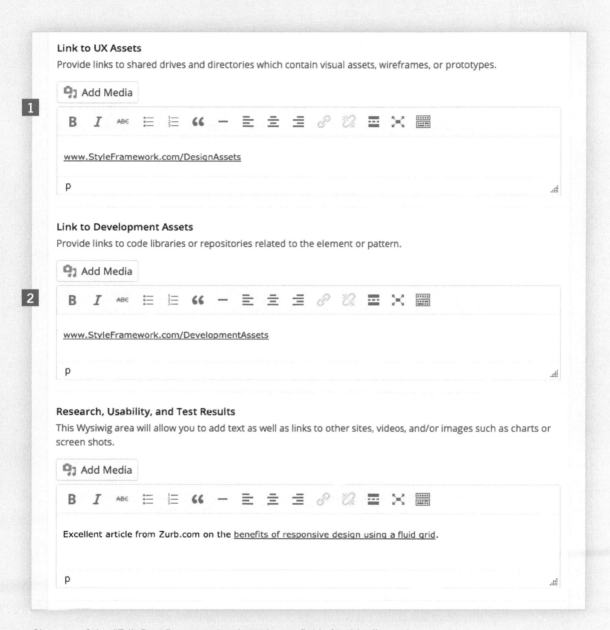

Close up of the "Edit Page" screen showing relevant fields for this discussion.

SEC 4   "I Need More Details"

So far, we have identified a standard, learned its proper use, and read details on how to build it. However, some standards will require just a few more pieces of information to validate their inclusion.

1 **Information on Research, User Testing, or Usability Reports**

Patterns and interactions only become standards once they have been proven effective. This section presents information and links to the user research, tests, surveys, and industry-accepted best practices which justify the use of this particular standard.

That is not to say that standards should not evolve. One of the benefits of a UX Style Framework is that anyone who would like to refresh a standard can use this section to locate the documentation that supported the initial decision. By reviewing this information, the organization can determine if it is time to update the standard or perform new testing.

2 **This Element May Also be Known As:**

In our earlier discussion on the guideline titled, "Say What You Mean" I gave an example of a costly miscommunication between a business owner and her development team. To promote a consistent vocabulary within the organization, this area will present the alternative names or terms used to describe this particular standard.

Not only will adding these other terms minimize vocabulary conflicts, it ensures this page will come up when one of your users searches for one of those alternative terms.

Additional details

1 **Information on research, user testing, or usability reports:**

Excellent article from Zurb.com on the benefits of responsive design using a fluid grid.

2 **This element or pattern may also be known as:**

Responsive Web Design, RWD, responsive framework, adaptive grid, responsive grid

3 **Related elements within this Style Framework:**

Modules

Screen shot of Section 2 from the "I Have to Build This" section on StyleFramework.com

3 **Related elements within this Style Framework**

If you are designing complex modules or new interfaces, this section may help you find all the components or interactions related to this standard. For example, let's assume you want to display data in a grid form, so you are looking at the Table/Matrix standard. If that is the case, you are also likely to be interested in sorting and filtering. A well crafted Style Framework will provide direct links to those related standards here.

Close up of the "Edit Page" screen showing relevant fields for this discussion.

CREATING OR EDITING THE "I NEED MORE DETAILS" SECTION IN WORDPRESS

1 **Adding Links to Usability Test Data and Best Practices**

A colleague of mine humorously calls this the "trust me, we've tried that already" section. In this area, you should provide links to past usability test results, customer surveys, specific market research, and any other sources which verify that this particular standard is superior to other tested solutions. Often, simply showing a list of tests is enough dissuade the "wannabe-designer" business owners from breaking standards in order to differentiate their products.

For each referenced source, you should include its title along with a brief description of the test or results. Since this information will often be in .pdf, Word, PowerPoint, Excel, or other formats, it is helpful to state the file format if you know it. All of this will be appreciated by the user as it helps quickly locate relevant testing information

If no actual tests were done (for example, on typography or color), use this area to include links to industry research or best practices, and explain the thought process or rationale behind the adoption of a particular element. While not as strong as actual testing, having this data quickly accessible will be invaluable when the inevitable debates arise.

2 **Entering Alternate Names for a Standard or Pattern**

It is worth the time to do a little research and peruse other publicly available libraries to find alternative terms for patterns. Pay very close attention to developer libraries, as there are a number of UX terms that migrated from the graphic design world that mean something totally different to an engineer.

3 **Entering Related Elements**

This section is fairly straightforward. Look to include items that are directly related, but do not overwhelm the user by showing casual connections.

SEC 5 — "I Want to Change This"

No matter how carefully crafted, all standards will evolve and change over time. The driving force behind the creation of UX Style Frameworks is to ensure all the work defining and documenting standards is not thrown away every 18-24 months. To achieve that goal, there must be a built-in, transparent mechanism for requesting changes, making decisions, and communicating updates to everyone in the organization who might be impacted.

The lower section of each page is focused on the governance of your standards, their evolution, and the process for making changes.

1 Owners and Governance

In an earlier chapter, we discussed the importance of having identifiable, individual owners for each standard. The owners are the subject matter experts for their assigned standard, and can answer any question about it. They are responsible for the accuracy of the information on this page, for answering questions, and for leading the change process when the standard is updated.

This area should include each owner's name as well as their email address. This will permit you to contact them directly via email, or better still, by using the Comments and Questions section at the bottom of the page (more to follow).

2 Other Information

And finally, this area is included for other information the owners believe might be relevant, yet which does not fall neatly into any of the categories above. Most of the time, it will read "Not Applicable" but it is included in case it is needed.

1 Owners and governance

UX or design owner
Marti Gold
Email: marti.gold@tonic3.com

Business or marketing owner
Marti Gold
Email: marti.gold@tonic3.com

Development owner
Marti Gold
Email: marti.gold@tonic3.com

2 Other information

Please include any other relevant information about this element or pattern:
Other information will go here

3 Comments & Questions

6 Comments

Mary Smith
February 8, 2015 at 8:34 pm   Reply Edit

Good morning! I was reading an article on button design which said that on sites using flat design, conversion improves if buttons are a slightly different shape than any other object on the screen. Since our buttons are currently rectangles, have we run any recent user tests to see if rounding the corners slightly will help users quickly identify these areas as buttons? Thanks for any input you can provide.

Marti Gold
February 8, 2015 at 8:36 pm   Reply Edit

Thanks for writing. We read the same article. I am currently checking with our User Testing Group to see if we can get on their schedule early next week to do a preliminary AB test.

Screenshot of the "I want to change this" section on StyleFramework.com.

Comments & Questions

3 6 Comments

Mary Smith
February 8, 2015 at 8:34 pm   Reply Edit

Good morning! I was reading an article on button design which said that on sites using flat design, conversion improves if buttons are a slightly different shape than any other object on the screen. Since our buttons are currently rectangles, have we run any recent user tests to see if rounding the corners slightly will help users quickly identify these areas as buttons? Thanks for any input you can provide.

Marti Gold
February 8, 2015 at 8:36 pm   Reply Edit

Thanks for writing. We read the same article. I am currently checking with our User Testing Group to see if we can get on their schedule early next week to do a preliminary AB test.

Mary Smith
February 8, 2015 at 8:43 pm   Reply Edit

Thanks very much for your reply. Hopefully we will discover a simple change that may help conversion. I look forward to seeing the results.

Marti Gold
February 8, 2015 at 8:48 pm   Reply Edit

Just wanted to give you an update. We were able to run an AB test which compared buttons which compared our current square buttons with buttons with a 5px border radius. The slightly rounded corners resulted in a 7% increase in clickthroughs. We are planning a second test to compare 5px radius edges with much rounder edges (12px or so) to determine if that makes identification even faster. We will keep you updated.

The test results for the most recent test are located at [insert URL here]

Marti Gold
February 8, 2015 at 8:53 pm   Reply Edit

CHANGE NOTICE: Based on recent test results, we have decided our Button Standards should be updated to specify 5px rounded corners for all buttons.

Details: A recent AB test showed that clickthrough rates increased 7% when button corners were changed from square to slightly rounded. Based on this result, we ran a second AB test comparing 5px rounded with 12px rounded corners. The second test showed the 12px rounded corners had a lower click rate than the 5px. As a result we are changing the standard to reflect the highest clickthrough rates as shown by testing.

Next steps: Each of the owners will communicate this change to our respective teams. Style Framework has already been updated so this change will be incorporated into work in progress. Development will work with QA to ensure this change is tested throughly before existing pages are updated. Target date to push this change live into production will be May 1, 2015. For more details on development rollout, please contact the development owner shown above.

The full report on the test, and our analysis of the numbers, can be found at [insert URL] here.

Mary Smith
February 8, 2015 at 8:58 pm   Reply Edit

Thanks very much for the update. I will share this information with my team as well.

Leave a Reply

Logged in as Marti Gold. Log out?

Comment

Post Comment

Conversation requesting a change to an existing standard.

3 **Comments & Questions**

The Comments & Questions section provides an easy to use, completely transparent mechanism for open discussions, sharing questions and opinions, and making changes to your standards. Anyone within the organization, in any department and any level, can express their views and submit ideas. Because it uses common social media conventions for adding and replying to comments, even the most non-technical users can participate.

Permitting transparent conversations (and sometimes debates) to appear on the actual standard page offers a number of very important benefits:

- Previous comments act as an FAQ. Simply by reading previously posted questions and answers, users often find the information they were looking for.

- It helps owners keep the standard up to date. If the same question keeps arising, the owners know that information should be added to the relevant section above.

- It eliminates any chance of "Design Dictatorships" as any decisions regarding changes will be documented in this area.

- When combined with the responsibility of each owner to communicate proposed changes to their own departments, it virtually eliminates the cry of, "no one informed us the change was going to be made." Anyone or any team can read the changes being proposed, and voice their opinion before the change is finalized.

- Discussions are usually quite polite and responses are well thought out, as everyone in the company knows who is writing.

The mechanism is actually very straightforward. Whenever a question or comment is submitted using the comment field, each of the owners are notified via email. The owners then visit the page and respond to the inquiry. To keep comments from growing too long over time, the owners have the ability to delete old or repeat questions.

CREATING OR EDITING THE "I WANT TO CHANGE THIS" SECTION IN WORDPRESS

1 **Adding Owners Names**

Depending upon the size of your company, you may have one to four separate names in the owners section. Even small companies usually have at least two, as the Business and Development owners are rarely the same person.

Although we explored the roles and responsibilities of owners in Chapter 3, be sure to remember that these names should not be executives nor department heads. While an Executive Vice President technically owns all the elements within the Style Framework, he or she will not be the person logging into the site to respond to inquiries, nor maintaining the pattern as it evolves.

The critical pieces of information to include are the owner's name and email address. Depending upon the size of your organization, your users may find it useful if you include the owner's title and phone immediately after their name.

2 **What Goes Into "Any Other Information"**

Although this field is intentionally left as a "catch-all", there are some common elements that may be important to those working with this standard. These include:

- Links to accessibility information. Not only the printed regulations, but color and contrast calculators, simulators for screen readers, and other tools.

- Links to any pertinent government or regulatory information

- Access to previously used standards, particularly those that have been recently retired.

Comment Area

The comment area is generated by users, so you will not need to add content there. You will, however, want to familiarize yourself with the tools to manage comments within WordPress.

Closer view of the "Edit Page" screen showing relevant fields for this discussion.

Name of UX Owner

Marti Gold

UX Owner email

marti.gold@tonic3.com

Name of Business/Marketing Owner

Marti Gold

Business/Marketing Owner email

marti.gold@tonic3.com

Name of Development Owner

Marti Gold

Development Owner email

marti.gold@tonic3.com

Any Other Information

Other information will go here

Please remember that you have the ability to completely customize your UX Style Framework to fit your company culture and workflow. Some of you may feel the sections outlined here contain too much information, while others may opt to expand the content areas to include even more detail.

But based on the success guidelines, in order to be effective, even the most spartan UX Style Framework should include:

- Name of the standard

- A brief description

- An image of the standard

- The problem the standard should solve

- Detailed specifications

- Links to relevant design and development assets

- The name of one owner

- A comments area

SAMPLE CONTENT

In this section, we will be examining examples of the content that might be included in your UX Style Framework. The emphasis in this area will be on the success guideline titled "Keep it simple."

These chapters will demonstrate how the number of items and the level of definition needed to ensure consistency in your interfaces may be far less than you expect.

Remember...

UX Style Frameworks do *not* define pages nor complex

components. UX Style Frameworks define *only*

the reusable, basic building blocks that will be combined

by your designers and developers to create

innovative, contemporary, and effective user experiences.

© nenovbrothers / Stockfresh

SAMPLE UX STYLE FRAMEWORK CATEGORIES

As mentioned previously, UX Style Frameworks are very flexible, and can be customized to fit a wide variety of organizational needs. These sample sections will help you evaluate and categorize various patterns that might be included in your own framework. They will also give owners a working recipe to facilitate research and compile the content for their respective standards.

SCAFFOLDING

These are the foundational items upon which everything else is built: Page dimensions, grids and modules, colors, and typography.

ELEMENTS

The basic building blocks of any site. These include links, buttons, containers, tables, lists, etc.

INTERACTIONS

This section will define the common interactions on your site: Scroll bars, light boxes, show-hide interactions, carousels, filtering and sorting, etc.

NAVIGATION

These are the elements that help your users move from page to page such as drop down menus, breadcrumbs, previous-next commands, and pagination.

FORMS

Perhaps one of the most critical areas of interface design, forms are the most direct way for users to communicate with you.

DISPLAYED CONTENT

Consistent data formatting is one of the most overlooked areas of user interface design. This area covers formatting of prices, dates, and times; tradenames; grammar; and spelling. It also addresses the presentation of graphic elements such as ratings, badges, image galleries, and maps.

ALERTS AND ERRORS

The patterns here will allow you to consistently communicate situations which need the user's attention—everything from page-level errors to battery life indicators.

FIXED ITEMS

Although our framework is focused on building blocks, a few complex components should be precisely defined to ensure global consistency. These include items such as headers, footers, and shopping carts.

OTHER

Includes additional standards for related products such as emails, advertising, and stand-alone mobile applications.

SCAFFOLDING

The team at Twitter Bootstrap coined the term "Scaffolding" for items in this category, and I think it describes them very well. These are the core foundational patterns that everything else in your application or web site is built upon. As such, while there aren't very many items within scaffolding, once defined they should *never* be broken.

Scaffolding is much like the basic interlocking rules of the popular plastic building block, Lego®. Even though Lego blocks come in all shapes and sizes, in order for the system to work, all blocks *must* follow the same specifications for connecting. Because these basic specs are never broken, the individual blocks can be combined and reused in limitless ways.

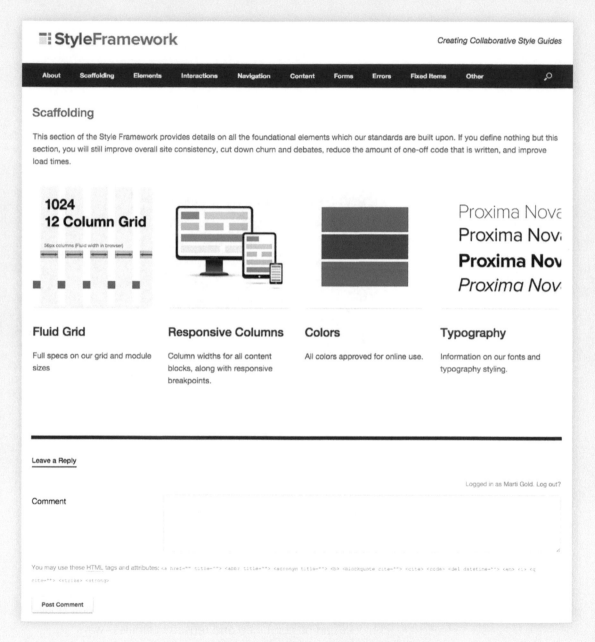

Screenshot of the Scaffolding Category Landing Page from StyleFramework.com.

WHAT TO INCLUDE IN SCAFFOLDING

PAGE DIMENSIONS AND GRID

Although slavish devotion to a grid is often criticized by graphic designers, most UX professionals and developers agree that using some form of grid is crucial for overall design consistency. A functional grid becomes even more critical when creating responsive layouts, as it determines how your various content blocks will behave when moved and resized.

COLUMNS OR MODULES

In order for your pages to take advantage of reusable components, your content should be sized to fit blocks which span multiple columns within your grid. This page will define those column spans, their sizes, and how those column blocks react when displayed at different widths when using a responsive layout.

COLORS

By taking the time to define your complete color palette in the scaffolding section, you eliminate the need to specify detailed color formulas for each individual element presented in the framework. It will also minimize the "eye-dropper curse" as designers and developers will quickly learn the precise color information they need is easily located on this page.

TYPOGRAPHY

Use this section to provide your typography specifications. This should include the fonts, weights sizes, and any special spacing considerations for body text, headlines, subheadings, bullet point lists, captions, etc. Again, by defining this in the scaffolding section, you will reduce the amount of documentation and CSS required to create page layouts.

Next, we'll examine each of these and further explain why they are included in this foundational group. I will also review the level and various types of information your owners may need to gather in order to effectively define them.

THE GRID

Whatever type of grid you decide upon, static or fluid, it should be the first element defined in your UX Style Framework. Much like the foundation of a building, the grid will have an impact on virtually every other element on your site. Using a grid system does *not* mean that your site's designs will become boring or boxy. It will, however, permit you to save time by incorporating reusable components and improve the overall aesthetics of your site by ensuring visually pleasing alignment of elements.

As you begin compiling all your existing specifications into one location, you may quickly discover that various departments across your company have adopted different grids. Some of these departments may want a fluid grid which resizes based upon the width of the browser window. Some will want a grid which maintains the same number of columns and gutters as it resizes, while others will want to keep a fixed column or gutter width but drop the overall number of columns when moving to smaller formats. Still others will push for three separate static grids— one for desktop, one for tablet, and one for mobile.

As difficult as it may be to reconcile these differences, it is imperative that your organization reach an agreement on a single grid system that everyone will use going forward.

A STANDARDIZED GRID WILL ENSURE:

- A consistent "framework" for all your pages that is designed to look good on all monitors and devices.
- Visual continuity from page to page.
- A greatly accelerated design process, as the grid's consistent measurements permit the creation of reusable templates and asset libraries which can be accessed by multiple departments.
- Reduced development time by permitting the generous reuse of HTML/CSS and Javascript elements for both content and interactions.
- Predictable and consistent behavior of responsive content blocks when pages are resized for tablet and mobile devices.

Fluid Grid

Last updated: January 25, 2015 at 0:32 am

A fluid grid is a layout structure which dynamically resizes to present the most elegant experience possible regardless of the user's current screen size. Often called a "responsive grid" or "responsive layout."

1024
12 Column Grid

56px columns (Fluid width in browser)

What problem does this element or pattern solve?

A standardized grid system reduces the number of subtle or major page layout variations across a site. This consistency creates visual rhythm, structural balance, and enhances the entire user experience by using predictable patterns. Adopting a grid system also expedites the entire design, development and maintenance process by permitting the development of reusable components and modules.

Fluid grids allow web pages to expand or collapse to fit the size of the current window, thereby ensuring the best user experience possible regardless of the device being used.

It applies to these platforms:

Desktop Web, Tablet Web, Smartphone Web

An example of this element or pattern in production:

www.StyleFramework.com

Screenshot of the Grid Detail page on StyleFramework.com.

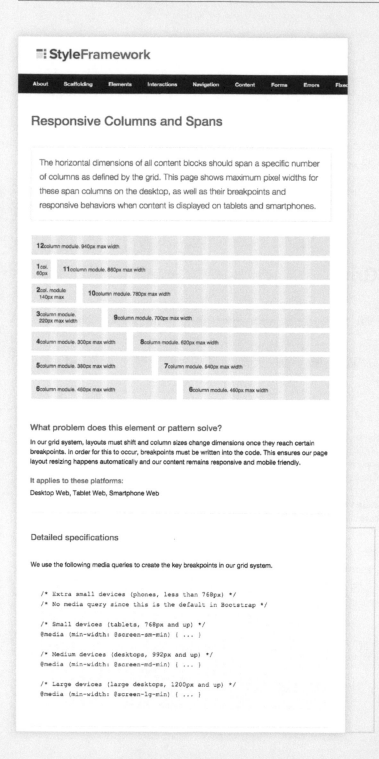

NOTE:
The Detailed Specification section of this page may include both layman's explanations of how the modules will resize and break, along with technical information for the prototyping and development teams. Therefore, when writing this section, be sure to identify and clearly separate the data for the two audiences.

COLUMNS AND MODULES

Once a grid is defined, the horizontal dimensions of all content blocks should span a specific number of columns as defined by that grid. The "Columns and Modules" page will present the pixel widths for each of these multi-column spans.

If your grid is responsive, your layouts will be required to shift —sometimes quite dramatically as the screen size changes.

In order for these fluid transitions to occur, the behaviors, dimensions and breakpoints for each module must be written into your standards. Without a single, definitive source, each department may establish its own rules. For example, one group may decide that side-by-side photos should simply shrink to fit the width of a smartphone screen, while another decides to wrap the images to display one on top of another. The result? Users will not see smooth nor consistent behaviors as they move from page to page.

This inconsistency will not only seem unpredictable and be irritating to users, it will require double the development and design effort.

On the facing page, you may notice that the example from StyleFramework.com has adopted a different name for this pattern. Remember, a UX Style Framework should display *your* organization's agreed-upon vocabulary for any particular pattern or interaction. Once decided, always refer to the element using its approved name, listing alternative or obsolete names in the "Also Known As" area. This is important for building a company-wide lexicon and minimizing mis-communications between departments.

© MPFPhotography / Stockfresh

COLORS

Although it is the most commonly searched element in any style guide, your site's color palette is regularly abused and ignored. As you begin compiling your UX Style Framework, you will probably discover hundreds of instances on your site where colors appear to be virtually identical, but the Hex or RGB values are very different. The quantity of these variations may be particularly staggering if your site use gradients regularly – you can thank the Eye Dropper Tool for that. Unfortunately, all those different codes result in unnecessarily bloated CSS code.

Once you have decided on a final color palette, you must accept that it may be infeasible to go back and standardize the colors on your existing pages. However, because those pages do exist, the temptation for developers and designers to fall back to old habits and use the Eye Dropper or Developer Tools will be strong. Therefore, your owners must actively communicate the location of this new and approved palette to their respective teams. It is particularly important that your QA department be aware of this page and reference it regularly, so that any color variants found on new pages can be corrected before going live.

TIPS FOR THE COLOR PAGE

- Provide both RGB formulas and Hex codes.

- Give the colors non-numerical names, such as "Charcoal" and "CompanyName Blue." That will allow owners to reference the colors in other sections of the framework without worrying about the inevitable typos that result when re-entering Hex or RGB codes.

- If a color is restricted to certain uses (buttons only, backgrounds only, errors only, etc.) be sure to tell your users.

- Include a "note" column near each color to address accessibility. Let your users know if a particular color passes WCAG accessibility tests (AA and AAA) when used in common combinations.

- If you use gradients, clearly define them here. If gradients are not permitted, state this as well.

- You may consider adding a "color balance" guide, to ensure that various pages do not use one color more prominently than another.

Screenshot of the Colors Detail page on StyleFramework.com.

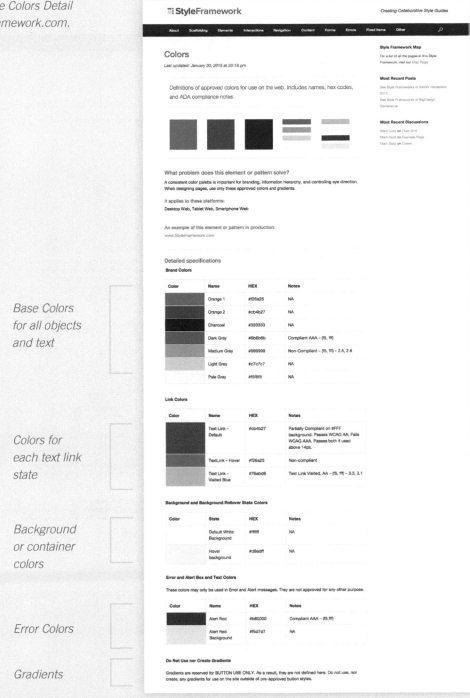

Base Colors for all objects and text

Colors for each text link state

Background or container colors

Error Colors

Gradients

Screenshot of the Typography page on StyleFramework.com.

Image of fonts with names

Font Names and weights

Information on web fonts

Font specs: sizes, weights, and line spacing

Offscreen: Links to all desktop and web fonts

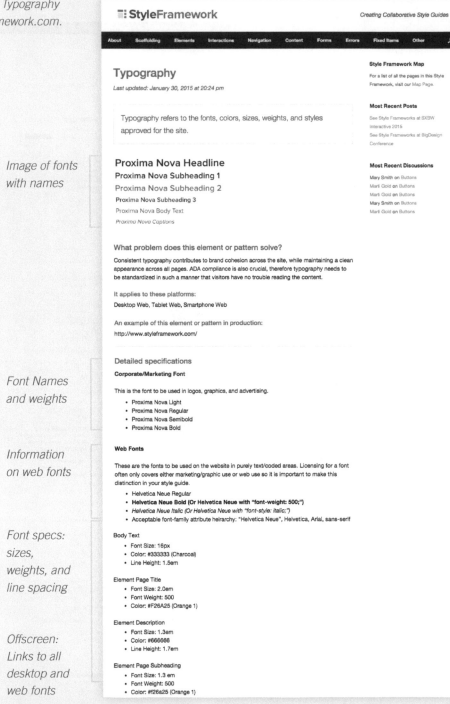

TYPOGRAPHY

Only a few years ago, the typography specifications of most websites could be defined using one word: Arial. That is no longer the case. As web fonts become more and more common, the online world is finally beginning to see genuinely interesting and beautiful typography.

However, very few people in your organization have even a basic knowledge of typography, let alone the visual and emotional impact it can have on pages. Therefore, as your users become more aware of different fonts and type treatments on web pages, this page will become increasingly important to the overall consistency of your work.

TIPS FOR THE TYPOGRAPHY PAGE

- If possible, design your entire Style Framework using the same font standards defined on this page. This include fonts, sizes, weights, colors, alignment and line spacing.

- In the Detailed Specifications section, work with your development owner to include the actual CSS and use the same class names that your developers will use. This not only ensures everyone is using the same vocabulary, it provides a fail-safe check for your QA department.

- In addition to providing the CSS specs for each font class, provide information on when each of the classes should be used in context. Provide links to existing pages as additional examples.

- Be sure to include the server location of both desktop fonts and web fonts in your links area so designers and developers can locate and download them.

- It is generally considered good practice to specify a base font size, and then specify all other font sizes as a percentage of that base size. Therefore, be sure to present your base font size first, and clearly identify it as such.

- In addition to the regular body text and subheadings, don't forget to specify special font treatments such as bullet points, numbered lists, captions, pull quotes, and table headings.

- If you use a web font for icons (such as FontAwesome), you should mention that here. However, you should also include those specs on a stand-alone icon page.

IF YOU ONLY DEFINE THESE FOUR ITEMS...

Take a quick look at your existing site and ask yourself the following questions:

- What would our site look like if every page followed the same grid?

- What if all our content boxes and photos were consistent sizes?

- What if, as users scrolled down the page, all our elements aligned vertically?

- What if all the button colors were consistent?

- What if all our headings were the same size and font from page to page?

- What if the spacing between our lines of text, and between various text blocks, were all the same?

- Would development be faster if our engineers could call preexisting, global CSS files rather than rewriting the most basic definitions over and over again for each page?

- Could responsive pages be ready for launch sooner if all our breakpoints were consistent?

- Would our pages make it through QA faster, with fewer bugs, if all our engineers were pulling their base code from the same pre-tested libraries?

If you do nothing else but define these four "Scaffolding" elements,
the overall visual design consistency improvements, reduction in
code required to create your site, and decrease in
overall development time will astonish you.

ELEMENTS

One step up from Scaffolding, you will find Elements. Elements are the distinct, core items that are combined with interactions to create more complex patterns and components.

In and of themselves, elements are very primitive. Yet on any individual web or application page, each one can appear many times. Because of this, it is critical that they be consistent—not only their visual design, but also the CSS classes that define them, and the code used to build them.

Remember that we are building a framework from simple to complex. If you compare scaffolding to DNA, then elements are the one-celled organisms.

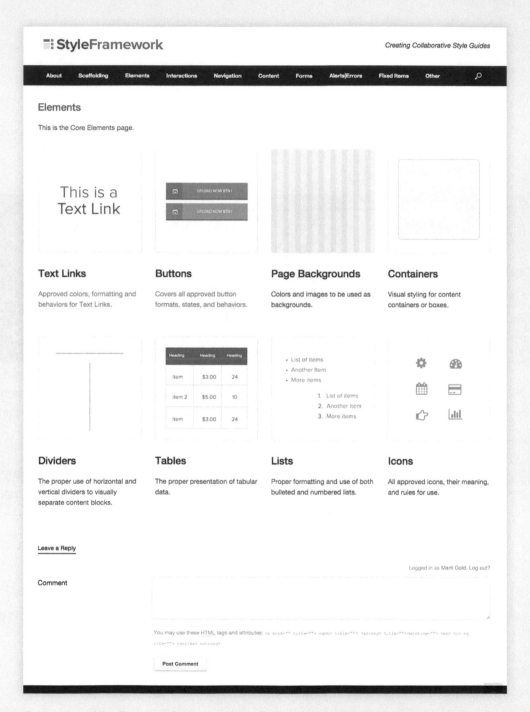

Screenshot of the Elements Category Landing Page from StyleFramework.com.

WHAT TO INCLUDE IN ELEMENTS

TEXT LINKS

One of the most simple, yet contentious elements on any website is the treatment of text links. Should they be underlined? Use a different color? How do they behave on hover? All these things will be defined here.

BUTTONS

Arguably the most inconsistent element on many sites, often due to competing product teams who insist their particular treatment increases click-throughs. This section will resolve those inconsistencies.

PAGE & BROWSER FILL BACKGROUNDS

Is the background color of your pages set to white or another color? Is there a pattern or a gradient? What is the browser fill color when the window is extended past your maximum page width?

CONTAINERS

All sites occasionally need to place content into boxes or containers in order to visually separate different sections of the page. Does your site put all content into containers, or just some? Do those containers have borders or shadows or rounded corners? What colors are permitted? Do you allow nested containers?

DIVIDERS

When containers are not used or are inappropriate, does your site use horizontal or vertical rules to separate unrelated content blocks? This section should spell out the proper use of dividers, their visual styling, and the guidelines to know when one should select a divider over a container.

TABLES

When information is best presented in chart or grid form, how is it formatted? Look here to find fonts, colors, borders, and other details to properly format tables.

LISTS

This section will cover the consistent formatting of both ordered and unordered lists. It includes bullet styles, colors, and spacing, as well as content rules to determine when you should use bullets or numbers.

ICONS

Your icon strategy is important, particularly when building responsive sites where space is limited. Use this page to clarify rules on when to use icons, and provide the list of approved icons and what they mean.

TEXT LINKS

Text links should be obviously clickable page elements, as they help users identify a direct path to related content. A user should always be able to effortlessly identify a text link whenever it is presented. That said, the blind adoption of traditional visual treatments for text links (always blue and underlined) is contentious at best. Therefore a clear definition of your text link styling is critical.

This is an example of a text link in its normal state.

This shows the text link in its hover or rollover state.

This shows the text link in its visited state.

This shows the text link in its active state.

This is a text link on orange in its normal state.

This is a text link on orange in its hover or rollover state.

This is a text link on orange in visited state.

This is a text link on orange in its active state.

This is a text link on charcoal in its normal state.

This is a text link on charcoal in its hover or rollover state.

This is a text link on charcoal in its visited state.

This is a text link on charcoal in its active state.

Specifications to consider:

- Your default text link color.

- Alternative link colors for use against secondary background colors, particularly in areas requiring reversed text (white text on dark backgrounds).

- Visual changes for all states. Do your links underline on hover only? Change color only? Or do both? Be sure to include mobile specs where there is no hover state.

- Define a distinctive visual style for disabled text links. This is particularly important if your website or application uses gray in your primary palette.

- Is hyphenation within a text link allowed?

- If possible, address content strategy and SEO concerns: Are text links permitted to be non-specific calls to action such as "click here" or "learn more"? Or should they always be descriptive?

- Do your links distinguish between targets? In other words, are anchor text links (which link to content on the same page) styled differently than off-page text links?

BUTTONS

Consistently formatted buttons will make click-ability obvious, draw a user's eye, and compel the user to take a specific action. Unlike a text link, buttons are not simply links to related or additional information. Instead, buttons should be used to trigger an interaction or reach the next major stage along a specific user path. As such, buttons should stand out from page content.

Specifications to consider:

- All background and text color combinations for your primary, secondary and tertiary buttons. Remember to check for WCAG compliance.

- Define the behaviors for buttons: Will you have hover state color changes, etc. Again, be sure to address responsive variations for mobile devices.

- The size and shape of buttons. Are button widths fixed or are they based on the text within? Are buttons with two lines of copy permitted? Is there minimum spacing on either side of the button's text? Will they have square or rounded corners, gradients, or shadows?

- Define all type treatments within your buttons: Font weight, text case, alignment, sizes, etc.

- Specify the minimum and recommended space surrounding buttons.

- Will your buttons contain icons as shown in the example here? If so, cover the rules for icon selection and display.

- Do not forget to define disabled button colors and behaviors and any rules for suppressing buttons.

- Cover any unique situations, such as different button treatments for advertisements, marketing message, alerts, or errors.

© liliwhite / Stockfresh

PAGE BACKGROUNDS & BROWSER FILLS

Although there are actually two separate items defined within this standard, they are very closely related and the information needed to define each is limited. The page background is where your application's main content will reside. The browser fill is the area displayed when a browser window is expanded past your maximum page width.

Specifications to consider:

- Will your page background and browser fill color be the same or different? Matching colors will give the illusion of centered content regardless of the browser width. Contrasting colors will define maximum page boundaries clearly *(see below)*.

- If the browser fill color is different than the page background, what is that color?

- Will you use page backgrounds or browser fill colors to visually define content sections, page types, sub-brands, or micro-sites?

- Are backgrounds limited to solid colors, or are patterns and/or images permitted? (If patterns or photos are permitted, be sure to show examples and provide links to approved images.)

Example of a striped pattern used as a browser fill

CONTAINERS

Containers are used to visually separate distinct subject areas within a page. By grouping related information into separate containers, the user can quickly identify content and interactions that belong together, minimizing confusion and improving comprehension. Ideally, your containers will align precisely to your grid, allowing the content within them to resize consistently in responsive layouts.

Specifications to consider:

- Define the approved shapes for your containers. Will they have square or rounded corners? Will your site present content in circle containers?

- Do you permit nested containers? In other words, can a box contain another box?

- Define any special effects such as shadows or borders. Be sure to specify the precise CSS settings to ensure consistency.

- If the containers have borders, are those borders on the interior, center, or exterior of the content box? (This is important for developers, otherwise two containers that are exactly the same numerical dimensions may appear to be different sizes.)

- Define your permissible colors. Are all containers white/gray or do you permit colors?

- Are reverse containers permitted (dark containers with white text)? If so, is there a minimum type size within reverse containers to ensure legibility? *Reminder: Always check for WCAG compliance.*

DIVIDERS & LINES

There are many occasions when you will need to visually separate two or more content blocks, but putting each into an individual container creates too much distinction. In these instances, you can use horizontal or vertical lines to create any necessary visual dividers between related sections of content. (*The example below presents four related pricing blocks separated by dividers, nested inside a single container.*)

Specifications to consider:

- Line formatting: Are your dividers solid, dashed, dotted? Do you have end-caps?

- What are acceptable colors?

- If you permit angles other than horizontal and vertical, specify those here.

- What are the approved divider widths in pixlels?

- What is the minimum spacing around each divider or line?

- Do you have specific guidelines governing when to use a divider vs. a container? Or is this at the designer's discretion?

- Can dividers also be used within containers?

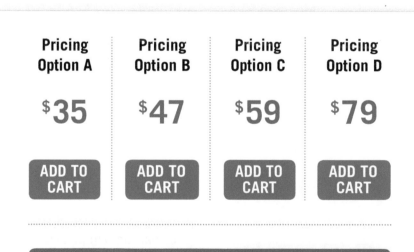

TABLES

Certain information, such as financial data and feature comparisons, is best presented in a table or grid format. However, these can be extremely problematic if you have a responsive website, as data formatting can be muddled when reduced from desktop to mobile phone screen widths. Use this section to clearly define your tables, when they should be used, and how to adjust their display on smaller devices.

Specifications to consider:

- Row and column background colors. Does your table have a consistent background color, or do rows or columns alternate between two shades?

- Row and column divider styling. This includes line colors and widths.

- How will wide-format tables behave when presented on responsive layouts?

- Spacing (padding) within individual cells.

- Any special typography rules. This is particularly related to alignment within the cells (left, centered, justified).

- Special formatting for numbers. Should numbers always align right even when the remaining cells align left? How many decimal places should be shown?

- Visual styling for table headings for both rows and columns.

- Rules associated with the use of tables. What type of content should be shown in table format?

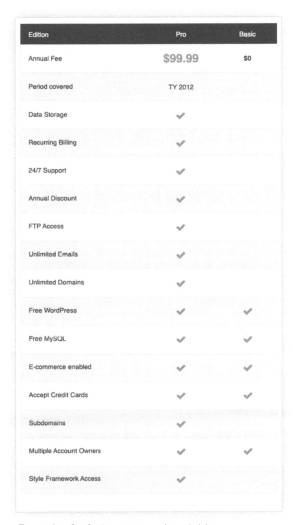

Edition	Pro	Basic
Annual Fee	$99.99	$0
Period covered	TY 2012	
Data Storage	✓	
Recurring Billing	✓	
24/7 Support	✓	
Annual Discount	✓	
FTP Access	✓	
Unlimited Emails	✓	
Unlimited Domains	✓	
Free WordPress	✓	✓
Free MySQL	✓	✓
E-commerce enabled	✓	✓
Accept Credit Cards	✓	✓
Subdomains	✓	
Multiple Account Owners	✓	✓
Style Framework Access	✓	

Example of a feature comparison table.

LISTS

It can be argued that the consistent visual treatment of numbered and bulleted lists should be included in the typography section. However, it may be more appropriate here, as this gives you the opportunity to explain when lists should be used as opposed to tables, as well as the content rules to determine if an ordered or unordered list is more appropriate. If you do opt to include list formatting in this section, remember to add a cross-reference link to typography.

Specifications to consider:

- Formatting for unordered lists: bullet shape or character, bullet color, size in proportion to copy, spacing between items, indents and line-wrapping, etc.

- Formatting for ordered lists: font and container colors, container shape, sizes, positioning of numbers within the shape, particularly if the list expands to 2 or 3 digits; spacing between items, indents and line-wrapping, etc.

- Content guidelines to determine when an ordered list or unordered list is more appropriate.

- Any differences in formatting when the list consists of single-line items vs multi-line items. Often, list items with multiple lines are given additional spacing between each bullet or number to improve legibility.

- Do your copy guidelines call for periods at the end of each list item?

Unordered List

- First item will go here.

- Second item should be placed here.

- This is the third item,which will wrap to multiple lines. Notice the spacing between bullet points is wider than normal line spacing.

- This is item four.

Ordered List

1. Item 1 will go here.

2. Item 2 should be placed here.

3. This is Item 3 which will wrap to multiple lines. Notice the spacing between bullet points is wider than normal line spacing.

4. This is item 4.

ICONS

Your icon page should present all the icons approved for use on your site and the rules surrounding their use.

Having a clearly defined icon strategy is particularly important due to the potential for icon misuse. Consider this example: Your icon strategy specifies that icons may only be used as a visual shortcut to describe functionality when space is limited. (e.g. display a printer icon to trigger a print dialog box when the word "print" will not fit.). Marketing requests an icon be inserted near a block of text to call more attention to that particular item on the page. In this instance, the icon is actually is being used as a small spot graphic. Under the rules of your icon strategy, the designer would know to reject Marketing's request, and would instead insert a small spot graphic or approved badge to achieve the desired goal.

The second benefit of a clear icon strategy is to prevent your pages from becoming overrun with icons—a disease I lovingly call "Severe Iconitis." Therefore, when selecting owners for this page, I recommend fairly senior employees who are not afraid to say "no", and have the ability to steer new icon requests toward more appropriate alternate solutions.

© cienpies / Stockfresh

ICONS - *CONTINUED*

© nmarques74 / Stockfresh

Specifications to consider:

- Present a clear icon strategy regarding when icons should, and should not, be used.

- Create a full list of all approved icons and their meaning.

- Are your icons based on web fonts (such as FontAwesome) or are they graphics?

- Present icon hover, active and visited states if applicable.

- If your icons are are fonts, include a link to the downloadable screen and web fonts, as well as the appropriate code formatting.

- If they are graphics, provide links to production ready graphics. Also, provide the location of the original files for the design team should the icon require editing.

- Include links to production ready sprites for developers.

- If an employee wants to create a new icon not on the approved list, include instructions for them to use the comment area. New icon requests should be viewed as a standard change request.

10

INTERACTIONS

This chapter introduces some of the basic interactions that permit customers to use your site. Although defining, and in some cases limiting, the number of interactions included in your standards will require careful consideration, adopting consistent patterns will improve overall user satisfaction. It is particularly important that the most common interactions, such as scrolling, behave precisely the same way from page to page. This will not only improve the user's experience, but also minimize the amount of code to be written and tested, decreasing your time to market.

I have opted to place interactions normally associated with forms in their own chapter. However, you may decide that all interactions should be included in this area. As always, select the best solution for your company.

StyleFramework   *Creating Collaborative Style Guides*

About   Scaffolding   Elements   Interactions   Navigation   Content   Forms   Alerts|Errors   Fixed Items   Other

Interactions

Interactions define all the various ways a user can change, manipulate or update our site to show more or different content. Unlike navigation which moves the user from one location to another, interactions normally occur on the same page.

Modal

Displays a container over the current page.

Accordion

A show-hide interaction that exposes one or more panels vertically.

Tabbed Panels

A show-hide interaction presenting one horizontal panel at a time

Scroll Bars

Facilitates scrolling horizontally and vertically.

Side Drawer

Show-hide interaction that reveals content from the left or right side.

Tool Tips

Click or hover over a trigger to display a content bubble.

Filtering

Applies criteria to reduce the items in a found set.

Sorting

Changes the display order of the data in a found set.

Media Players

Controls the playback of audio or video media.

Carousel

Steps through content panels one at a time.

Leave a Reply

Comment

Logged in as Marti Gold. Log out?

Post Comment

Screenshot of the Interaction Category Landing Page from StyleFramework.com.

WHAT TO INCLUDE IN INTERACTIONS

SCROLL BARS

Scroll bars are called whenever your content exceeds the size of the window. This area will describe the rules for their use, as well as their visual styling and behavior.

TABBED PANELS

Like accordions, tabbed panels only show one content area at a time, but follow traditional file-folder visual metaphor. Panel names are shown in a horizontal row across the top of the dynamic content area.

ACCORDIONS

Accordions expand vertically and permit one content area to be shown at a time.

CAROUSELS

Carousel interactions permit users to browse through a fixed set of items, displaying one at a time. Items are normally images, but can also be text or a combination of the two.

SIDE DRAWERS

Formerly limited to mobile sites, the side drawer panel is becoming increasingly common on desktop sites. This interaction permits new content be presented by "sliding in" from the left or right side of the screen.

MODALS

Modals display content in a container, disabling the rest of the page. Modals prohibit the user from interacting with the page below until an action is taken.

FILTERING

Whenever a large data set is presented, filtering controls allow users to eliminate items from the set, creating a smaller and more relevant subset of data.

SORTING

Unlike filtering, sorting does not reduce the actual size of a found data set. It merely rearranges the order of the display of the data based on specific criteria.

MEDIA PLAYERS

Media players permit users to control video, audio or other rich media on a site.

TOOL TIPS

These are small instructional containers which are displayed by clicking or rollover.

OTHER INTERACTIONS

Needless to say, the interactions above are a small subset of your available options. Check here for other common interactions you might consider including in your Style Framework.

SCROLL BARS

Although they are one of the most common interactions, you should include scroll bars in your UX Style Framework definitions. Scroll bars are normally activated whenever there is more information than can be displayed in the viewable area of a screen or container. They are most commonly vertical, but can be horizontal as well.

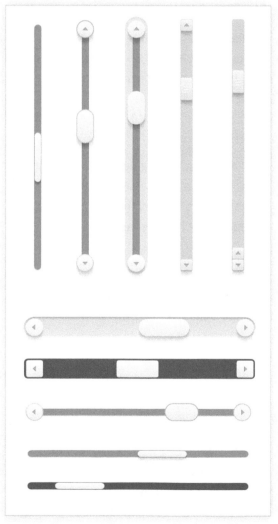

© ildogesto / Stockfresh

Specifications to consider:

- Do you have custom visual styling for your scroll bars or will your applications always default to the browser or OS styling? If you require custom styling, be sure to include all specifications, both visual and behavioral. Also define if there are any instances when default scroll bar styling is acceptable.

- When should scroll bars appear? When are they intentionally suppressed?

- Are horizontal scroll bars permitted, or vertical only? If vertical only, be sure to provide your users with a link to interactions which present horizontal movement such as carousels.

- Do you permit scroll bars within containers such as modals, tabbed panels, or accordions?

TABBED PANELS

Tabbed panels provide access to content when space is limited and a page refresh is not desirable. They are normally displayed as a horizontal row of links, placed in individual containers, that just above the content. Clicking a link displays its associated panel. The downside to tabbed panels is that labels must remain short and formatting for responsive sites can be problematic.

Specifications to consider:

- Be sure to include when to use Tabbed Panels over Accordions or other types of show-hide interactions.

- Define any restrictions on the tab titles. Is there a maximum character count? Can tab titles be two or more lines?

- The visual styling for the tabs. Are they a fixed width size or dependent upon the width of the entire panel? Is there spacing between them? Do they have rounded corners?

- Define the visual styling for the panel's main content areas. Typography specs, background colors, borders, shadows, etc.

- Is there a recommended size or a maximum amount of content permitted within each panel?

- Carefully define responsive behaviors, as the presentation of tabbed panel content can be problematic on smaller screens.

| Tab Panel 1 Heading | **Tab Panel 2 Heading** | Tab Panel 3 Heading |

Tabbed Panel 2 Heading

Tortor, eget ornare urna. Duis varius tellus eros. Donec odio arcu, rutrum ac rutrum eget, bibendum ac enim. Phasellus hendrerit iaculis purus. Aliquam sit amet molestie odio. Sed commodo dictum consequat aenean in est.

Dolor sit amet, consectetur adipiscing elit. Aliquam vitae fringilla augue. Maecenas in lectus lorem. In et accumsan mi. Aenean vestibulum nisl eu arcu viverra iaculis. In hac habitasse platea dictumst. In vehicula diam et mauris imperdiet aliquet. Phasellus hendrerit iaculis purus. Aliquam sit amet molestie odio. Sed commodo dictum consequat

© neirfy / Fotolia

ACCORDIONS

An accordion (or accordion menu) is a grouped set of collapsible panels that allow a user to access a great deal of content within a limited amount of space. Panels are individually expanded by hovering or clicking. Expanding a panel usually causes the others to collapse, showing only one panel of content at a time. However, they can be configured so all panels stay open until closed by the user.

Specifications to consider:

- Do your accordion panels show only one content panel at a time, or can they be expanded to show multiple panels simultaneously?

- Do panels expand on click, or on hover only? It is best to select one interaction method in order to increase the learnability of your site.

- Is there a limit on the amount and type of content within each panel? This will ensure that one panel does not display significantly more information than any others.

- Define the visual styling for the accordion container, title bars and content areas.

- Call out any changes in the hover and active states for your panels. This includes the typography and colors for both the title and main content areas.

Accordion Panel 1 Expanded

Dolor sit amet, consectetur adipiscing elit. Aliquam vitae fringilla augue. Maecenas in lectus lorem. In et accumsan mi. Aenean vestibulum nisl eu arcu viverra iaculis. In hac habitasse platea dictumst. In vehicula diam et mauris imperdiet aliquet.

Accordion Panel 2 Closed

Accordion Panel 3 Closed

Accordion Panel 1 Closed

Accordion Panel 2 Expanded

Sed velit congue viverra. Sed porta mattis luctus. Curabitur feugiat pharetra sem eu iaculis. Phasellus venenatis volutpat arcu id placerat. Aliquam fringilla ligula eu purus lacinia at volutpat nunc malesuada. Nunc a augue ac orci tempus commodo.

Accordion Panel 3 Closed

Accordion Panel 1 Closed

Accordion Panel 2 Closed

Accordion Panel 3 Expanded

Tortor, eget ornare urna. Duis varius tellus eros. Donec odio arcu, rutrum ac rutrum eget, bibendum ac enim. Phasellus hendrerit iaculis purus. Aliquam sit amet molestie odio. Sed commodo dictum consequat aenean in est. Donec odio arcu, rutrum.

Accordion Panel example
generated by Adobe Muse

CAROUSELS

Another way to display multiple content elements within the same space is a carousel. One item, or set of items, is displayed at a time. The interaction controls often double as visual cues to indicate the total number of items in the set, the current item being displayed, and if the user is moving forward or backward with the set. Carousels can display images, text, or any other combination of permitted elements.

Example showing the first and second panels of a three-step carousel

Specifications to consider:

- Do you have a limit on the number of items that can be included in a carousel?

- What are the visual cues for the number of items in the set? Will you use thumbnail graphics of each image? Simple graphic shapes? If one of these visual cues are clicked, is the corresponding image immediately displayed?

- On the visual cues, how will you indicate the current image being displayed?

- Will your carousel automatically rotate through the items if the user does not interact with the tool? If so, how long is the delay before this rotation starts? If the user does interact, does the automatic rotation stop completely?

- Will you include "previous" or "next" controls? If so, where are they located and how are they styled? When the user reaches the end of the set, will "next" take them back to the start?

MODALS

A modal is a child window or panel that requires the user to interact with it before they can return to the parent page or application. They provide a way for users to access additional information without leaving the current page. Once a modal is activated, the page below is disabled until the user takes an action or cancels the modal. This interaction is also commonly known as a lightbox or overlay.

Specifications to consider:

- Carefully define the rules regarding when to use modals. They are quite easy to implement, so they have the potential for abuse.

- Define the maximum size of the modal. Generally it is best to cover no more than 60% of the screen.

- Explain how a user can close a modal. Clicking outside the container area? Clicking a close box? Or both?

- Visual styling of the content container.

- Define the background color and opacity. It is normally best to set opacity so the page below is obscured but visible. By doing this, the user will realize they are still on their desired page, but must interact with the modal in order to continue.

- Can your modals display multiple-step content or panels? If so, what other patterns can be used as a modal?

SIDE DRAWERS

Side drawers are panels that transition from the left or right side of the screen and display content or navigation options. When fully extended, a side drawer can either overlay the content on the main page or push it to the side. Like a modal interaction, the side drawer must be closed in order for the user to continue interacting with the page below. While initially used primarily on mobile devices, side drawers are becoming more common on the desktop.

Specifications to consider:

- Do you permit side drawers on desktop applications, or are they limited to touch devices only?

- What visual affordance should be used to alert the user that a side drawer is available? While three horizontal lines (often called "a hamburger") is the common icon used, many user experience experts believe a word such as "menu" should also be included.

- How is the side drawer activated and/or closed? Swiping or clicking? If swiping, how is the drawer controlled on non-touch devices?

- How should the sidebar be positioned when it is fully expanded? Is it permissible to cover global navigation or other header items?

- What is the maximum percentage of the screen that a fully expanded drawer may cover?

© BigDesignDallas.com
Uses Vertoh Wordpress Theme

FILTERING

Although it is one of the most common interactions, filtering is often misunderstood by users. When a large data set is presented, filtering allows users to enter criteria to *eliminate non-matching items* from the found set. User confusion can enter when filtering criteria and sorting criteria appear to be the same. As a result, these two interactions should be carefully considered, and tested together, to ensure that the function of each one is clear.

Specifications to consider:

- Location of filter controls. Traditionally, filtering controls appear on the left side of the screen, but that may not be the best solution for your application.

- Do you permit multiple types of controls? Radio buttons, check boxes, drop downs, range sliders, and other common form interactions can be used.

- Does the data automatically refresh when any filtering control is used? Or should the user set all their filters, then hit a "submit" button to view the results?

- For complex filtering, will you provide the user with a reset button?

- When filters are applied, how are those shown to the user? Common presentations include a breadcrumb-like trail near the top of the screen, or highlighted filter names.

- If you have many filters, should you present them using accordion or other show-hide interaction to save space?

Complex filtering options
as presented on Amazon.com

SORTING

Unlike filtering, sorting a large block of data does not reduce the actual number of items within the data set. Sorting merely rearranges the display order of the information. For example, filtering by price allows users to remove all items costing over $100, thereby reducing the found set from 5000 to only 50. Sorting by price will take the subset of 50 items, and re-arrange those items from lowest to highest price.

Specifications to consider:

- The location of the sorting controls. Traditionally, sorting controls are often placed in a horizontal row, just above the data display.

- Do you permit multiple sorting operations? For example, can a user sort by zip code and then sort within that zip code by price?

- How are sorting controls displayed? Are they clickable table headings? Do those labels present small arrows to show ascending or descending sort order? Or are your sorting options presented in a select list?

- Your standards should define the default sort order for all initial displays of data.

- When results are sorted, how is the current sort order communicated to the user?

- If you permit multiple sorting operations, how are those controls presented? Options might include a right rail, a modal, or a side drawer.

MEDIA PLAYERS

Although they include more complex interactions, media players are listed here because of the unique nature of the content presented within them. Due to the popularity of YouTube, users have come to expect common iconography for specific controls, and it is wise not to stray far from those conventions. However there is still a great deal of flexibility when it comes to visual styling.

Specifications to consider:

- Will you have separate players for video and audio content?

- Will the content within your media player begin playing automatically, or will the user be required to touch a "play" button.

- Carefully define the positioning, visual styling, and behavior of all controls.

- Will your videos play in the main content area, or launch within a modal?

- Will the player display a static image until the play control is clicked? Or will the non-playing screen be a simple, solid color?

- Will you permit users to control the volume within the player itself, or will you rely upon their current system settings? Will you include a mute button?

- What aspect ratios will your video player support? If you play a video with a different aspect ratio, what is the color of the container background?

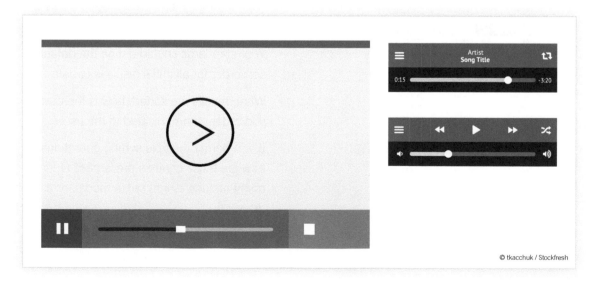

© tkacchuk / Stockfresh

TOOL TIPS

Tool tips are small containers of text which appear whenever an object might benefit from a short written description. Tool tip copy is normally a short verbal phrase that provides a brief instruction or clarification. Historically, tool tips appear whenever the mouse is hovered over a specific area, but touch devices have recently introduced changes to this interaction, requiring more detailed definitions.

Specifications to consider:

Kitten Sleeping ⊗

Tool tips can be activated by hover or by clicking. Because mobile devices do not have a hover state, you should provide a close mechanism for using overlays or tooltips.

- Because of the potential for overuse, carefully define the rules for implementing tool tips. Tool tips should never be a crutch to compensate for poor usability nor ambiguous content.

- Define the presentation of tool tips. Do they display when a user hovers over the trigger or do they require a click? How is "display on hover" handled on touch devices?

- How will your tool tips close? Are they timed to automatically disappear? Do they vanish on roll-out? Again, how is this handled on touch devices?

- Do they include a small visual affordance (trigger) to alert the user that a tool tip is available?

- Can they be triggered by a text link alone? If yes, how does this link differ visually from a traditional text link?

- Is there a limit to the amount or type of content that can be presented within them? Can you have scroll bars within a tool tip?

- How will the expanded content area be positioned on the screen in relation to the trigger? Does the expanded area always extend toward the center of the screen regardless of the position of the trigger?

- Fully define the visual styling of the tool tip container and fonts—color, borders, shape, shadows, font sizes, alignment, etc.

Cat photo by Death to Stock. Tooltip example created in Adobe Muse.

OTHER COMMON INTERACTIONS

Obviously, this chapter presents only a small subset of basic interactions that might be defined on your site. Scanning the many pattern libraries available on web will give you excellent ideas. But remember—only include interactions that are both necessary *and* unique.

Here are more interaction suggestions that may apply to your framework.

Expand-Collapse Transitions

Used when an object is not of primary importance, but must be visible in a smaller form. Clicking the object will toggle it between its larger and smaller state.

Drag and Drop Interactions

Rearranging modules or adding/uploading content by dragging it into a new location using the mouse or finger.

© tkacchuk / Stockfresh

Zoom In / Zoom Out

These interactions permit users to enlarge or reduce text or images. The commonly recognized visual affordance for this interaction is a magnifying glass with "plus" or "minus" signs within it.

Panning

Permits the users to reveal hidden areas of a large image by dragging the image within a content window.

Endless Scrolling

When the user scrolls down the page and reaches the end currently loaded content, the system dynamically loads additional content without a page refresh.

Looking for form interactions? No worries. They are grouped together in the "Forms" Chapter.

NAVIGATION

Navigation controls define the many ways users can move around and access the information on your site. Due to the relatively recent proliferation of mobile devices and responsive design, site navigation has become increasingly important and complex. This section will examine a few specific patterns normally associated with navigating from page to page.

While you are building your UX Style Framework, use this opportunity to not only ruthlessly evaluate your existing navigation patterns, but to update them for the next generation of mobile-friendly sites.

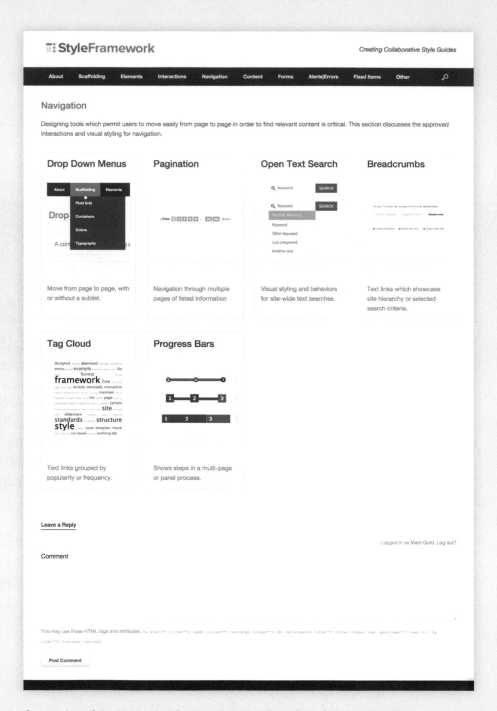

Screenshot of the Navigation Category Landing Page from StyleFramework.com.

WHAT TO INCLUDE IN NAVIGATION

PAGINATION

Pagination controls are needed whenever there are too many items or search results to fit comfortably on a single page. These controls will allow the user to rapidly move between related pages.

BREADCRUMBS

When used for navigation, breadcrumbs show where a particular page is located in the site's hierarchy. However, they may also be used to display sorting or filtering attributes selected by the user. We will discuss both options.

TAG CLOUDS

A tag cloud is a grouping of links, normally styled so the font size of each link is determined by the relevance or popularity of its associated content.

OPEN TEXT SEARCH

Open text search patterns allow users to enter keywords into a text box and search your entire site for specific topics of interest. Search results are often displayed on a new, specially formatted page.

PROGRESS BARS

Progress bars are used to show a progression of steps in a multi-screen process. In addition to providing visual cues on the user's progress, each step can be clickable, permitting navigation between the sections.

DROP DOWN MENUS

Drop down menus can be either horizontal or vertical, and are used to navigate to various sections of a website. Often, clicking on the menu heading will expose a sublist of links to related content.

PAGINATION

Your website may need to effectively present a large number of items—this is particularly true for e-commerce sites offering thousands of products. Pagination is helpful whenever there are too many items to display comfortably on one page. Pagination controls serve two purposes: 1) they allow users to move quickly between pages to locate specific items, and 2) they provide a visual cue on the total number of items available.

Specifications to consider:

- Most important question: Are you going to use pagination, or will your site incorporate endless scrolling (an interaction which continually loads additional results or content as the user continues to scroll)?

- If you opt for traditional pagination, where will the controls be positioned? Above the content, below it, or in both locations?

- Will you show all available page numbers? If not, what are the range breaks?

- Will you include page numbers or only previous and next controls? Will you include a link to the first and last pages?

- What is the visual stying for the page numbers? You should define the normal, active, and hover states.

- Should you include an additional "current item count" indicator, such as "showing Items 20-29 of 310?"

- Will you include a "skip to page xx" control which permits users to use a text box to enter a specific page number?

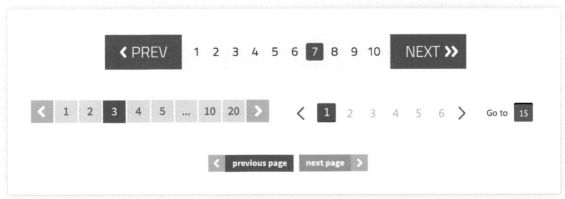

© sabelskaya / Stockfresh   © tkacchuk / Stockfresh

BREADCRUMBS

Breadcrumbs may have two purposes. When used for navigation, they clarify the location of a particular page within the site's hierarchy. When sorting or filtering search results, breadcrumbs display the attributes selected by the user. Traditionally, breadcrumbs are shown above the page content as a single line of text links whose labels match a corresponding page or attribute.

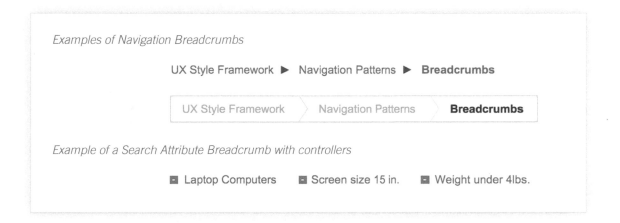

Examples of Navigation Breadcrumbs

UX Style Framework ▶ Navigation Patterns ▶ **Breadcrumbs**

| UX Style Framework ⟩ Navigation Patterns ⟩ **Breadcrumbs** |

Example of a Search Attribute Breadcrumb with controllers

◧ Laptop Computers   ◧ Screen size 15 in.   ◧ Weight under 4lbs.

Specifications to consider:

- If you need both navigation and search attribute breadcrumbs, consider the pros and cons of defining these two separate standards using different names. It may not advisable to have two unrelated functions sharing a name simply due to their similar visual styling.

- If you use both types, establishing consistent locations to help differentiate these functions becomes important. Navigation breadcrumbs should be closer to the page title, while attribute breadcrumbs should be near your content.

- Will the two types of breadcrumbs have different visual styling?

- Consider the visual dividers for your breadcrumbs. Navigation breadcrumbs frequently use an ">" symbol, while attribute breadcrumbs often use a colon or other non-directional symbol.

- Will your attribute breadcrumbs include a delete controller? Or will the user always be required to add or delete search criteria using traditional filtering controls?

TAG CLOUDS

A tag cloud is a grouping of text links where the font size and/or styling of each link is determined by the perceived importance or popularity of its associated content. Tag clouds are helpful to users who want to browse the most popular topics on your site. They also allow quick visualization of the subjects and type of content you offer. They should not be used to show information that has a strict hierarchy.

Specifications to consider:

- Define user stories covering when and how a tag cloud should be generated. Will the links be dynamically generated based upon user activity (such as recent or popular searches)? Or will they be pre-determined by the actual content on your site?

- How will the links be ordered? Options include alphabetically, randomly, by weight with the largest text near the center, or clustered by related subjects.

- Will you present common phrases or single words only?

- What is the minimum and maximum number of links that can be shown in a tag cloud?

- Is the tag cloud container a fixed size, with text sizes expanding or contracting to fit within that area? Or, are text links displayed in predefined sizes, allowing the tag cloud container to expand?

- Will the text links vary in size or font as well as color? Will words or phrases always be converted to lower case?

OPEN TEXT SEARCH

Even though your site will include global navigation, users may want to search for specific items using keywords. Open text search patterns normally consist of label, a text field for entering desired search terms, and a "submit" button. Search results are often displayed on a new page that has unique formatting and functionality. While technically a form, open text search is a common method of quick navigation and may fit best in this section.

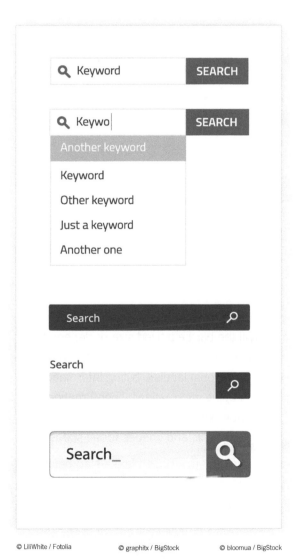

Specifications to consider:

- Where will your open text search area be displayed? Best practices indicate it should be considered a global feature, and occupy a consistent location site-wide.

- Will you offer auto-suggest or auto-complete functionality? *(More details on this pattern in Chapter 13.)*

- Is the user required to press a "submit" button to generate search results, or will hitting "enter" or "return" perform the same function? Or, will the results begin to dynamically update as the user types?

- Will you use an external label which says "Search" or will the search label appear as ghost text within the text field itself? Be sure to confirm accessibility coding guidelines if you decide upon ghost text.

- Fully define the size and visual styling for all the elements: input box, labels, keyword text, and trigger buttons.

© LiliWhite / Fotolia   © graphitx / BigStock   © bloomua / BigStock

PROGRESS BARS

A progress bar should be used to set expectations for the activities and length of a multi-screen process. The active state of the bar allows users to see precisely where they are within that process. Ideally, each bar will also be clickable, permitting users to easily navigate to any step. Progress bars should be presented as soon as the user begins the process and have a one-to-one relationship between each bar and its corresponding screen.

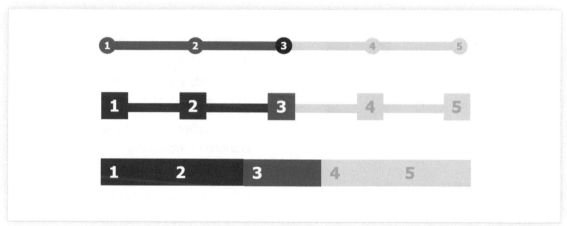

© tele52 / Stockfresh

Specifications to consider:

- Clearly define when a progress bar will be used. Ideal applications include complex forms such as registrations, or training wizards which present step-by-step instructions to complete a task.

- How will steps be broken down? While it is ideal to have one bar for each screen, a 1:1 relationship is not necessary so long as the steps are clear.

- Will users be permitted to move forward or backwards at will?

- Define the visual styling and behaviors. Will the bar be a fixed size or dependent upon the number of steps? Will it include instructional labels ("billing information", "shipping information", "confirmation") or numbers only? Include information on colors, fonts and shapes for all states.

- If the user must complete a step before being permitted to advance to the next, how will disabled steps be displayed?

DROP DOWN MENUS

Drop down menus are used to navigate among sections of a website when space is limited. These menus often appear near the top of the page but can be inserted within the content area itself. Generally, they are presented as text within a box or container (also known as a trigger area). Hovering or clicking the trigger area will expose a sublist of selectable, related items.

Specifications to consider:

- Does the menu expand to show the sublist on hover or click? Keep in mind that if you are building a responsive site, a hover state will not be available.

- If the sublist is exposed on click, will it collapse on rollout if the user does not select a sub-item?

- Will you permit multiple tiers of sublists?

- Does the sublist appear from the bottom or the side of the trigger?

- Do you permit drop down menus within content area, or only in header areas?

- If you are building a responsive site, be sure to define the behavior of your drop down menus for mobile phones and tablets. As the screen width decreases, will they change orientation (from horizontal to vertical)? Or will they be converted into a drawer or fly-out interaction?

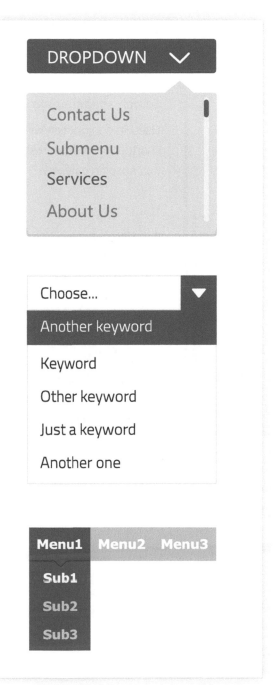

© sabelskaya / Stockfresh

OTHER NAVIGATION STANDARDS

As with other chapters, this area presents only a few of the navigation options available to you. Here is a short list of other patterns you might consider.

Search shortcut drop downs

Used in conjunction with open text search, a shortcut drop down restricts the search results to a specific category.

Home Page Link

It is always advisable to provide your user with some way to return to the home page of your site. Traditional practice states your site's logo should always be link to the home page, but there are many other options.

Footer Links

Although your global footer area will be covered at length in a later section, it can be a valuable navigation tool for users.

DISPLAY CONTENT

I was quite torn on how best to describe this section—I finally settled on "Display Content." Although interactions and elements are important, they are meaningless without content. This chapter focuses on the standards surrounding the presentation of words and images to your users.

Because the content on each site is unique, the topics within this section of your UX Style Framework may vary greatly from my examples. However, this area is where inconsistency frequently rears its ugly head. Worse, because these items are subjective, they also trigger a great deal of unnecessary churn. Better to define them once, and be done.

StyleFramework

Creating Collaborative Style Guides

About | Scaffolding | Elements | Interactions | Navigation | Content | Forms | Alerts|Errors | Fixed Items | Other

Content

"Pushed" content is the information we present to our users. This includes everything from our headlines and product descriptions, to reviews and prices, to photo captions and legal disclaimers. All of our content should use our brand voice, follow consistent spelling & formatting, and display accurate trademarks. Some content, such as ratings, may not be written, but nonetheless should follow established guidelines.

Our Logos

StyleFramework
StyleFramework
StyleFramework
StyleFramework

Access logo specification, rules for use, and downloadable files.

Spelling & Grammar

email

login

User Name

Check here for company approved spelling and grammar.

Dates and Times

USA: MAR 03 2014

World: 03 MAR 2014

12:01 PM

Proper formatting of dates and times used on our site.

Currency & Numbers

CURRENCY EXAMPLES

Correct	Incorrect	
$ 24.00	$24.00	$24
$ 2,325.00	$2,325.00	
$ 24.00 (USD)	USD $24.00	
$ 0.36	$0.36	36¢
$ 24.00 (CAN)	CAN $24.00	
15.29 €	€15.29	

Ensures proper display of prices and numbers.

Trademarks

Trademark™

Registered®

Servicemarks℠

Proper spelling and formatting of all our brand names.

Photography

Approved photo styling and links to image libraries.

Charts and Tables

GRAPH TITLE
INCREASE +37%
QUANTITY
23,589
COMPARISON VISUALIZATION
75% vs 25%

Visual styles for charts, tables, and infographics.

Maps

Functions and styling for maps. Direction formatting.

Social Media Content

Display of social media icons, trade names, and interactions.

Leave a Reply

Logged in as Marti Gold. Log out?

Comment

Post Comment

Screenshot of the Display Content Landing Page from StyleFramework.com.

WHAT TO INCLUDE IN DISPLAY CONTENT

LOGOS

Covers the use of your company logo, and provides links of approved logo sources. In addition to the primary logo, you should include logos for branded products and divisions.

TRADEMARK LIST

This reference page should present a list of all your trademarked names with their precise, legally approved spelling AND appropriate symbols.

FORMATTING DATES & TIMES

Addresses the wide variety of acceptable options for formatting of dates and times. Numeric formatting, time zones and offsets, abbreviations, capitalization, sequencing.

FORMATTING CURRENCY & NUMBERS

The consistent and clear display of numbers and pricing is particularly important for e-commerce sites, as ambiguous or inaccurate formatting can dramatically impact sales.

SOCIAL MEDIA LINKS

Many people forget that social media icons represent quite large and successful brands, and as such, have restrictions on their use. This area should cover the guides for using social media brand assets.

CHARTS & GRAPHS

The presentation of data in chart or graph format can be highly impactful, but without guidance on visual styling and approved types, your web site could quickly become a hodgepodge of wildly varying chart formats.

MAPS & DIRECTIONS

In a mobile and responsive world, interactive maps not only help customers find you, but are also a valuable decision-making tool. Be sure yours are consistent.

PHOTOGRAPHY AND IMAGE STYLING

In a word of constantly changing images, a picture speaks a thousand words. Define your brand's photography style here.

SPELLING & USAGE

Your Framework should also include a page that covers approved spellings, common content usage, and grammar for your site. This will eliminate the question, "Is it email or e-mail?"

LOGOS

You may find it interesting that logos are included the Display Content chapter rather than in the Scaffolding section. While logos are a critical component of your brand, they are not a foundational element on which other items are built. In addition to your primary logo, your company may also have logos for individual brands or product lines. All rules surrounding their use should be covered in this section.

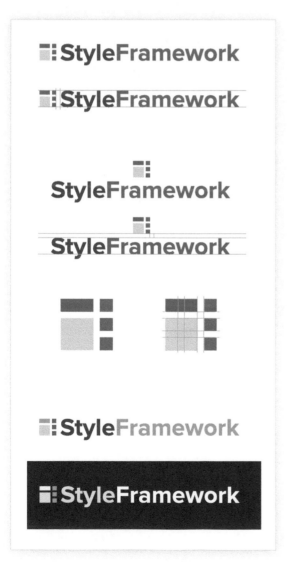

Specifications to consider:

- The exact location of your company's downloadable logo assets. Care should be taken to emphasize that logos must *never* be recreated, and should only be taken from company approved graphic assets.

- If your logo has approved variations (i.e. vertical, horizontal, or reversed version), you must present and define the guidelines for the proper use of each one.

- Specify the minimum size for each of your logo variations and at what point designers should use a text treatment instead. Specifying a minimum size is necessary to ensure your logos remain legible.

- Include rules regarding the minimum space that must surround your logo.

- It advisable to include examples of logo variations or distortions that are *not* approved. This includes color changes, removing parts of the logo, changing the aspect ratio to fit fixed spaces, and other common errors.

TRADEMARKS AND COPYRIGHTS

It is critically important to protect your company's trademarked products by using the correct spelling, capitalization, and legal mark placement whenever your brand names appear. Including this information within your UX Style Framework will provide the entire company with a single, definitive source to locate this important information.

AirDrop®	iMac®
AirPlay®	iMessage®
AirPort®	iMovie®
AirPrint™	iPad®
Apple®	iPad Air®
Apple logo®	iPad mini™
AppleLink™	iPhone®
Apple Pay™	iPhoto®
AppleScript®	iPod®
AppleShare®	iPod shuffle®
AppleTalk®	iTunes®
Apple TV®	iWork®
Apple Watch™	Keychain®
Bonjour®	Keynote®
Charcoal®	LaserWriter™
Cocoa®	Launchpad®
EarPods™	Mac®
FaceTirne®	MacApp®
Final Cut Pro®	MacBook®
Finder®	MacBook Air®
FireWire®	MacBook Pro®
GarageBand®	Macintosh®
iBook®	Mac OS®
iLife®	Mac Pro®

Examples of Apple's trade names and marks

Specifications to consider:

- All your brand's registered trademarks which must include the ® symbol.

- All your brand names that are pending registration, requiring the use of a trademark symbol (™).

- All your names that are pending registration and require a service mark symbol (℠).

- Your brand's official wording and formatting for all copyright notices (©).

- Your logo artwork should include the appropriate positioning and size of each legal mark in relation to its corresponding logo.

- All of the above for each of your major suppliers and partners.

- Rules for displaying any required content author credits (stories, photos and videos)

- Include proper trademark treatments for major competitive brands if you regularly use those names in product comparisons.

DATES AND TIMES

Another area which commonly displays inconsistent formatting on websites and applications is the display of dates and times. This is not only limited to numerical formatting, but also the use of abbreviations, capitalization and sequencing. If your site has an international audience, accurate displays of date and time may be critical.

Specifications to consider:

- Do you use a 12-hour or 24-hour clock?

- Show multiple examples of approved time formats. This should include hours and minutes, use and capitalization of AM and PM, and the display of seconds (if applicable).

- Do you display dates with the month first (USA) or day first (Global)? If your site is international, does date formatting switch based on the user's detected country?

- Do you include the day of the week?

- How do you show time zones or offsets?

- Do you display years as 4 digits or only the last 2 digits? Are months displayed as numbers or words?

- Be sure to include all approved abbreviations for months and days of the week. It is advisable to show examples of unapproved versions as well (e.g. MAR vs. Mar. vs. March). If you permit two or more display options, be sure to add guidelines defining when each should be used.

Time

Correct	*Incorrect*
1:00 PM	1:00pm 1:00 p.m. 1:00PM
12:00 AM	12:00am 12:00 a.m. 12:00PM
4:15:35 AM	4:15 AM, 0:35 sec

Special information
Formatting for Time Zone: 12:00 AM (EST)
Midnight is 12:00 AM; Noon is 12:00 PM
We do not display time in 24-hour format (18:00)

Dates

Correct	*Incorrect*
WED (3 char caps)	Wed Wednesday
JUL (3 char caps)	Jul July JULY
07/31/2015	7/31/15 07/31/15 07.31.2015

Approved Combination Formatting

JUL 31 2015	WED JUL 31 2015
07/31/2015	WED 07/31/2015
12:30 AM, WED JUL 31 2015	

CURRENCY AND NUMBERS

To put customers at ease, particularly on e-commerce sites, it is important to have a consistent and clear display for currency and pricing. As the web becomes more globally focused, the need for clarity increases due to the wide range of global price formats, formal terminology for denominations, and the fluctuating nature of conversion rates.

CURRENCY EXAMPLES

Correct	Incorrect
$ 24.00	$24.00 $24 $24.00
$ 2,325.00	$2,325.00 $2325.00
$ 24.00 (USD)	USD $24.00
$ 0.36	$0.36 36¢
$ 24.00 (CAN)	CAN $24.00
15.29 €	€15.29
£ 8.35	£8.35
£ 8.35 (GBR)	GBR £8.35
¥ 1,235	¥1,235 ¥1235

PHONE NUMBERS

Correct	Incorrect
(214) 555-1212	214-555-1212
	1-214.555-1212

General Notes:
- *Place a space between the currency marker and the number.*
- *Use commas to separate thousands*
- *Use 2 decimal places when applicable*
- *Only use country designations (USD) when mixing denominations on the same page.*

Specifications to consider:

- Define the visual styling for your prices, in all accepted denominations. This list may be much longer than you expect, so provide clear labels and examples that can be scanned and identified quickly.

- Provide direction on spacing issues if your site dynamically updates pricing for various countries. The horizontal space required to display a price in US dollars without wrapping may be much less than the space required when displaying prices in pesos.

- Do you display decimal points of the currency unit, or round up to the nearest unit? If so, how many decimal places?

- If your site regularly creates comparison pricing tables or grids, you may want to define the visual styling and behavior of those tables here, and add a cross reference to the tables/grids page.

- Do not forget to define other common number formats such as phone numbers, distances, weights, or measures if you use them regularly.

SOCIAL MEDIA DISPLAY

At the time of writing this, virtually every website includes at least a few external links to social media and other external sites. Because these external services have their own trademarked icons and badges, care should be taken not to violate those trademarks. Use this area to define the proper use, positioning and sizes of social icons or links to external sites.

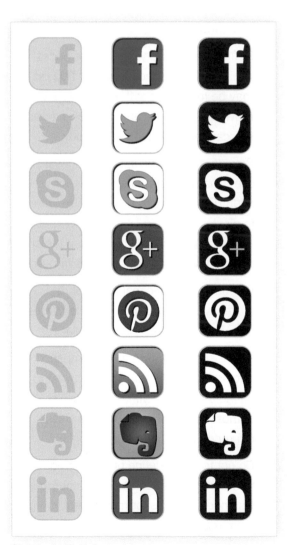

© tanya_ivanchuk / Stockfresh

Specifications to consider:

- Show clear examples of all approved visual treatments for social media links.

- Provide links to repositories where social media icons or other brand assets are stored. Be sure to state that for consistency and the integrity of both your brands, it is unacceptable to go to the web and simply right-click any social media example and place it on your site.

- Give examples of the various positions on a page where social media links can be placed.

- If social media icons can be placed into context on the page, be sure to show an example of its visually stying and any necessary placement rules.

- Be sure to include the proper spelling and trademark designations for each Social Media source name for text treatments or alt-tags.

CHARTS AND GRAPHS

There are hundreds of different types and styles of charts and graphs, ranging from simple bar charts to highly complex infographics. Use this page to define the various types of charts that can be displayed on your sites, their visual styling, and rules to help designers select the best type of chart to present various data types.

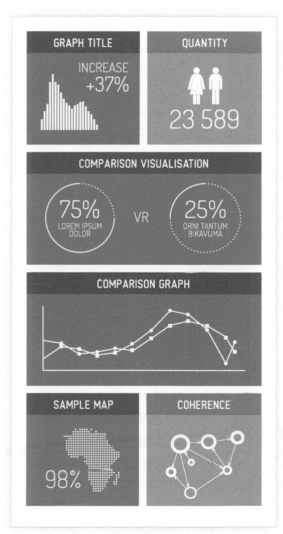

© orson / Stockfresh

Specifications to consider:

- All approved chart formats: Pie, bar, line, scatter, map, etc.

- Approved colors for use in charts. Be sure to specify the presentation sequence of the colors (one-color charts are red only, two color charts are red and blue, three color charts are red, blue and yellow; etc.)

- Visual stying for your chart labels and graphs. This includes line widths, line colors, fonts, font sizes, and spacing.

- Do your charts display the actual number on or near its related segment (e.g. overlaid on the corresponding section of a pie chart)? What happens when the visual section is too small to display the number?

- Do your charts present legends or keys? How are they formatted?

- Are your charts flat or do they have 3-D effects? Do you permit gradients?

MAPS AND DIRECTIONS

With the proliferation of mobile devices, interactive location maps have become a mainstay of many applications. Although the basic functionality may be controlled by an external API, in most cases the number of activated interactions and visual styling are highly customizable. This page, which may turn out to be quite long, should accurately define your company's strategy for the use and consistent behavior of maps.

© kraska / Stockfresh

Specifications to consider:

- Brief information on the Map API provider, along with direct links to that providers support area so developers and designers can get additional information.

- Multiple examples of approved map styling and interactions within the API. Origin points, target destinations, points of interest, route lines, keys, legends, zooming, panning, etc.

- Visual affordances which trigger maps. This includes text, icons, and thumbnails. Do these affordances contain static or dynamic content?

- How are maps shared or printed from within your interface?

- Visual styling of map containers. This should include containers, borders, titles, location of print and share icons, etc.

- Interactions which display maps. Can maps appear inside a modal only? Should they be presented in an accordion or other expandable area? What about small maps inside a tool tip?

PHOTOGRAPHY AND IMAGE STYLING

The importance of imagery, and its impact on the effectiveness of your site, cannot be overstated. A single image truly can speak a thousand words—both positive and negative. Ironically, many organizations who spend millions on offline branding routinely ignore the photography on their website. In order to protect your brand, use this page to educate your colleagues on the vital importance of professional imagery.

Images from Death to Stock Photo

Specifications to consider:

- An explanation of the brand strategy behind your photographs and images.

- Examples of the acceptable and non-acceptable images, with clear explanations. For example: "This photograph is not allowed because it is black and white. We only permit full color images to be used."

- A link to a library (internal or approved stock vendor) with previously approved images. It is very important that these images be quickly scannable or searchable.

- Examples of items to address: Do you permit illustrations or do you limit images to photographs only? Do you permit black & white or tinted photography, or full color only? Can photos include obviously applied filters? When showing people, can they be "camera aware" (e.g. looking the camera)?

- Do you have maximum or minimum sizes for photographs?

SPELLING AND USAGE

Having a quick-reference guide for spelling and usage is important whenever employees are writing content visible to customers. The idea is to ensure consistency and promote a "single voice" across the site. This page will save time and resources by providing instant answers when questions arise about grammar, punctuation, or recommended spellings.

Spelling

Correct	*Incorrect*
email	e-mail
log in	login, log-in
user name	username
web site	website

Capitalization

Correct	*Incorrect*
Gone with the Wind	Gone With The Wind
CA	California, Ca

Punctuation

Correct	*Incorrect*
Item, Item, and Item	Item, Item and Item

Abbreviations

Correct	*Incorrect*
St. Ave. Hwy.	Street, Avenue, Highway

Specifications to consider:

- List of common words with controversial spellings: Does your company use "email" or "e-mail"? "Login" or "Log In"? "Username or User Name"?

- Capitalization. Are headlines in all caps? If you use title case, do you follow the rule that articles and prepositions four letters or less are left in lower case? ("Gone With The Wind" vs "Gone with the Wind".)

- Punctuation. Do you use the Oxford comma? (Warning: this discussion may approach the level of a religious debate.) Do you place periods at the end of bullet points?

- Use of abbreviations. Defining this area is far more difficult than it sounds, as many sites permit common abbreviations such as "Ave." for "Avenue",

- Use of Acronyms. Do you permit the use of "FAQ" or should "Frequently Asked Questions" always be spelled out?

- Links to the company's approved style guide and brand voice materials.

13

FORMS

Although the internet contains a wealth of data, users must supply information in order for web sites to return content that is relevant. To do that, they need forms.

Although it can be argued that many of the elements in this special "forms" chapter could easily fit into previous sections, your internal users may be able to locate form input standards more easily when they are grouped together.

When reviewing this chapter, please remember that UX Style Frameworks are not meant to define complex patterns. The form elements here will only give you examples of basic input types and what is needed to define them. Combining these base elements into ever-evolving and relevant patterns is what will keep your framework alive.

StyleFramework
Creating Collaborative Style Guides

About | Scaffolding | Elements | Interactions | Navigation | Content | Forms | Alerts|Errors | Fixed Items | Other

Forms

In order to ensure users can easily interact with our site and provide us with information, consistent and reliable forms are critical. This section covers the basics of form creation, and addresses consistent styling and behaviors.

Field Labels

Name:

Enter Name

Email:

Enter Email

Position and visual styling for field labels.

Text Input fields

Enter your email address:

Email Address

Email Address

Behaviors and visual styling for basic open text input fields.

Mandatory Fields

Full name: *(mandatory)*

Street Address

Zip Code: *(mandatory)*

Proper designation and markers for mandatory form fields.

Auto-Suggest

Keyword | SEARCH
Another keyword
Keyword
Other keyword
Just a keyword
Another one

Provides contextual hints when entering data into text fields.

Check Boxes & Radio Buttons

✔ First category
✔ Category #3
✔ 5th category
✔ Category nm.

Proper use and styling of check boxes and radio buttons.

Select Lists

Select a Category
Scaffolding
Elements
Interactions
Navigation
Forms
Alerts and Errors
Fixed Items

Permits users to select from a pre-populated list of responses.

User Names & Passwords

👤 Username

🔒 Password

••••••••

Behaviors and visual styling for basic open text input fields.

Dates, Times, and Ranges

◄   January   ►

Sun Mon Tue Wed Thu Fri Sat
         1   2   3   4   5
6   7   8   9 10 11 12
20 21 22 23 24 25 26
27 28 29 30 31

Options for accurately entering dates, times, and ranges.

Currency and Numbers

123   321

1988 ⌃ ⌄

Entering and formatting numbers, currency and ranges.

Ghost Text

e-mail

Enter your email address:

EMAIL

Text within fields providing hints regarding field content or formatting.

Leave a Reply

Logged in as Marti Gold. Log out?

Comment

Post Comment

Forms Category Landing Page from StyleFramework.com.

WHAT TO INCLUDE IN FORMS

FORM FIELD LABELS

There is often great debate regarding the visual styling and positioning of form labels. Your label text can have a quite dramatic impact on the effectiveness and usability of your forms.

TEXT FIELDS

While the most basic of all input field types, the open text fields can present unique challenges when it comes to validating the data entered.

MANDATORY FIELDS

This section covers the visual styling and positioning of mandatory field indicators.

AUTO-SUGGEST

When a user begins entering text into a field, a select list appears with suggested words or phrases. This page will cover the rules surrounding auto-suggest functionality.

CHECK BOXES & RADIO BUTTONS

While radio buttons limit users to only one response, check boxes are used when the user may select multiple choices. You must set rules to determine when and how each of these formats should be used.

SELECT LISTS

Select lists restrict the potential input responses for form fields. These are quite valuable for reducing validation errors when choices are limited.

USER NAMES & PASSWORDS

Although technically text fields, user name and password fields have particular restrictions and behaviors which will be addressed here.

DATES, TIMES, AND RANGES

This page covers these common, yet complex input types. Options discussed here are designed to minimize validation errors.

NUMBERS AND NUMERIC RANGES

There are multiple options for entering numeric data ranging from open text fields to select lists to numeric steppers.

GHOST TEXT

Form fields often place labels or formatting hints inside text fields which disappear when the user activates that field and/or begins entering data. Here are options to help you evaluate the pros and cons of this practice.

OTHER INPUT FORMS TO CONSIDER

A list of other options you may want to add.

FORM FIELD LABELS

Those who have been caught in debates over the positioning and content of form labels can attest that very few topics can create as much churn. Ironically, tests show that users don't have any real preferences when it comes to label formatting so long as the labels are clear and it is obvious which field is being referenced. What is important, however, is consistency and behavior across pages and devices.

Specifications to consider:

- Consider the typography for form field labels. Is it consistent or different from other copy on the site? If different, is it clearly defined on the typography scaffolding page?

- Finalize the alignment and positioning of labels in relation to their corresponding fields. Recommended positioning may be closely tied to your maximum label length.

- Will your company place labels outside the form fields or within them (Ghost Text)? This discussion may be more contentious than many heated political debates.

- Be sure to specify any label positioning shifts when switching between devices.

- If additional information or hints are required (for example, "passwords must be at least 6 characters"), where will those be positioned in relation to the field or label? How will they be formatted? Will they be placed inside tool tips?

- Cross-reference the page which contains information on form field errors, mandatory field designation, and validation.

TEXT FIELDS

A basic input field for any form is the straight text entry field. While arguably the most versatile, this field type is also the most prone to input errors. As a result, defining input validation rules, and when validation will occur, may occupy a great deal of attention. Technology to minimize input errors, such as auto-complete and ghost text, will be discussed shortly.

Specifications to consider:

- Carefully define the visual styling of your text input boxes. Provide specifications on background color, borders, interior shading, font sizes, font color, etc.

- Will your text form fields be set to a consistent width? Or will the width vary, providing a visual cue for the proper input (i.e. zip code fields with maximum 10 characters)

- For multi-line input fields, such as comments, how will scrolling be handled?

- Be sure to provide cross-referenced links to the other necessary standards required to create fully functional forms. These might include validation, error messages, form labels, auto-suggest, and others.

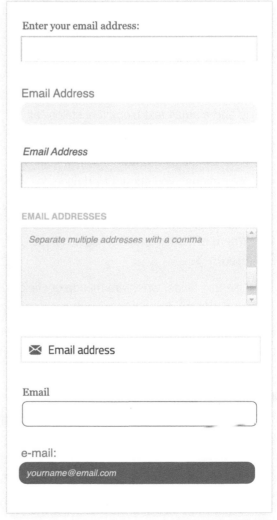

Examples of text field visual styling.

© Multiple Designers / Stockfresh

MANDATORY FIELDS

Many User Experience professionals believe, "if a form field isn't mandatory, it should be eliminated as there's no need to ask the user for unnecessary information." However, just as many marketing professionals feel differently—they want to collect as much information as the user is willing to provide. When defining this pattern, you must balance these two positions to find your site's conversion "sweet spot."

Specifications to consider:

- First, you must determine if all the fields presented on your forms are mandatory. If so, then a mandatory field designator will not be necessary. However, you may want to add a small text block that states "all fields" are mandatory.

- If certain fields are mandatory while others are optional, you should alert users to that fact. What is the visual styling for the mandatory designator? Is it text or an icon? Where is it positioned? What colors are used?

- Like text fields, when are mandatory fields validated?

- As mentioned earlier, be sure to carefully cross-reference related form standards and provide examples of working forms to help your designers and developers maintain consistency.

Full name: *(mandatory)*

Street Address:

Zip Code: *(mandatory)*

👤 Your name   *

✉ Email address   *

Write your message...

© liliwhite / Stockfresh

All fields must be completed.

Full Name:

Email Address:

Examples of mandatory field treatments.

AUTO-SUGGEST

To speed up input and minimize data entry errors when using open text fields, particularly on mobile devices, auto-suggest can be a valuable feature to include on your forms. As the user begins entering text, a select list containing suggested terms will drop down. The user merely clicks the desired term, the drop down vanishes, and the search field is populated.

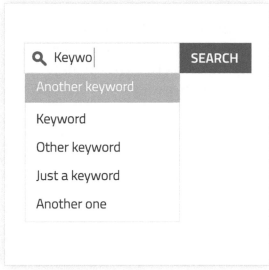

© sabelskaya / Stockfresh

Specifications to consider:

- There is huge potential for internal vocabulary confusion surrounding the terms auto-suggest, auto-complete, and auto-fill. The latter are often used to describe a browser setting which automatically populates multiple fields with saved data (such as complete shipping addresses). In order to avoid misunderstandings, use this area to clearly differentiate which term is used to describe which behavior.

- When presenting your suggested responses, must the user physically click or touch the preferred response from a select list? Or will suggestions be made with ghost text as the user types?

- If the user makes an apparent spelling error, will the application make an automatic correction (i.e. iPhone Auto-Correct)? Can the user disable this feature?

- Are your auto-suggest behaviors different for desktop and mobile devices?

CHECK BOXES AND RADIO BUTTONS

Although their functionality is very different, there seems to be ongoing confusion regarding the use of radio buttons and check boxes. Radio buttons should be used when two or more options are mutually exclusive and the user can choose only one. Check boxes are used when the user may select multiple choices. Use this section to identify which to use when, as well as their visual styling and placement.

Specifications to consider:

- You may find it advantageous to place radio buttons and check boxes on the same standards page to help business owners more accurately differentiate between them.

- Be sure to address instances when a single checkbox should be used. This is often necessary for a user confirm their understanding or agreement to important terms and conditions. Although there is only a single response, radio buttons cannot be used because they cannot be unchecked.

- When using radio buttons, will one item be pre-selected to ensure the field validates? Or will the initial display be blank to avoid inaccurate responses if the field is overlooked?

- As with other form items, include any special formatting or visual styling instructions that are needed.

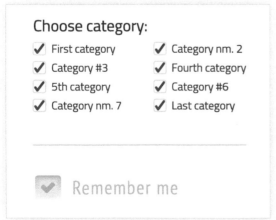

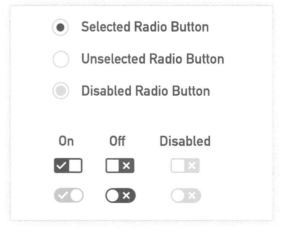

© liliwhite / Stockfresh

SELECT LISTS

Unlike drop-down navigation menus which move users from page to page, select lists are drop downs which restrict the potential input responses for form fields. While a select list can contain a large number items, only one value can be selected. This field type is commonly seen when users must choose a single response from values commonly shared by all users, such as state, country, or credit card type.

Specifications to consider:

- Consistency is key when defining select lists. The fields which present select lists, their visual styling, labels, label order, and values should be perfectly consistent from form to form.

- What is the sort order for your select lists? Is it always alphabetical? Or are more popular selections placed near the top to minimize the need for scrolling? Again, consistency is important. If you present a list of countries in alphabetical order in one form, you should not present that list on another with your home country listed first.

- If your form is restricted to a small area, will you specify a fixed size for your select list and permit scrolling within it?

- How are select lists displayed on various mobile devices?

- Do you have special visual styling, such as fonts and visual affordances for your select lists? Or do you always use the browser or OS default styling?

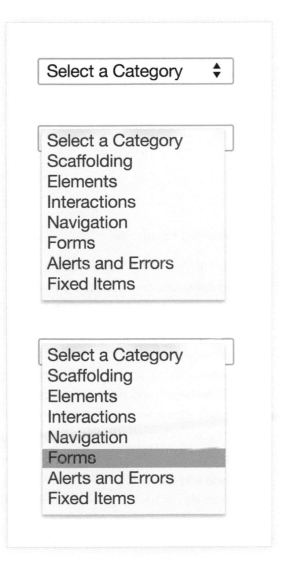

USERNAMES & PASSWORD FIELDS

Usernames and password fields have unique requirements and formatting which warrant their own page. Because of the complexity of the log-in process and its numerous use cases, many sites direct their customers to a stand-alone log-in page. Conversely, just as many present log-in tools on multiple pages. Regardless of the option you select, use this section to define universal behaviors and styling for these two related field types.

👤 Username   Enter username or registered email address

🔒 Password   ●●●●●●●●

☐ Display password   Forgot password?
✓ Remember me

© liliwhite / Stockfresh

Specifications to consider:

- If you have a special "log-in" pattern in the Fixed Items section that details business rules such as these, you should cross-reference it here.

- When setting up a new account, how will you communicate special requirements for valid usernames and passwords such as minimum character count or the need for a symbol or number? (Ghost text? Tool tip? Secondary label line?)

- Will you add "remember me" functionality so users do not have to re-enter their username or password? How is this information saved?

- Will your site mask password entry, or display the password characters? If display, must the user check an opt-in box? If the opt-in box is selected, is that setting saved?

- How many failed password attempts do you permit before a user is locked out? How long is the lockout period?

- If you have user-selected usernames, how is the user told his/her name is available?

- Do you use a system such as Captcha to prevent automated login attempts? If so, how is it implemented?

DATES, TIMES, AND RANGES

There are many accepted ways for users to enter dates and times. Select lists are common for both, while calendar pickers are used frequently for to specify dates. However, the interactions become more complicated when the user must specify a range between two dates or times. Due to its complex nature, this is a standard which may require more senior owners who understand all the variations or Use Cases that need to be addressed.

Specifications to consider:

- Will you use calendar date pickers or select lists? Select lists take up far less screen space, but calendar-pickers showing the day of the week may be more helpful.

- When using calendar pickers, be careful to follow local customs for starting the week on Sunday versus Monday. This will minimize user mistakes.

- When using calendar pickers for a date range, should you show two months at a time to cover ranges which start one month and end in the next? Will the range between the start and end date be highlighted? What is the interaction for changing the start or end date?

- Define the visual styling for all calendar picker controls, such as advancing months or years.

- When selecting times,how will you address time zones? When specifying time ranges, how will you communicate total time along with shifts in time zones or days (such as air travel)

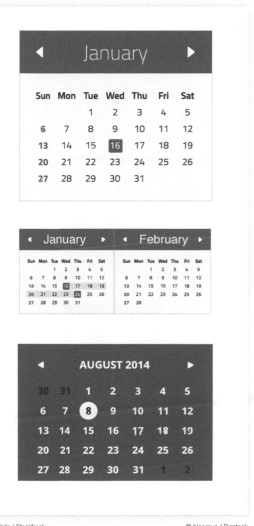

© liliwhite / Stockfresh

© bloomua / Bigstock

NUMBERS AND NUMERIC RANGES

While not as complex as dates and times, the options for entering numbers ranges include open text fields, range sliders, select lists, and numeric steppers. Often the best entry method may be determined by the context of the response needed, as well as the input device (touch, mouse or keyboard). Because of this, care should be taken to define the approved entry methods as well as the rules surrounding when each should be used.

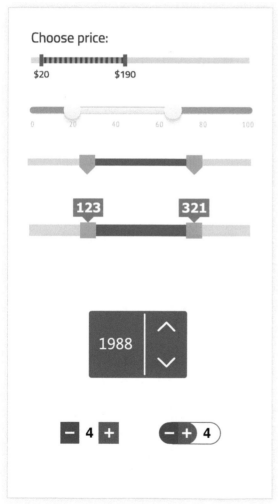

© liliwhite / Stockfresh
© sabelskaya / Stockfresh

Specifications to consider:

- Will you have wildly different numeric ranges in your forms that may require completely different input formats? For example, a hotel convention reservation system may need to ask the total number of event days (generally a single digit number) *and* the estimated number of convention attendees (which could be in the tens of thousands). In cases like this, you should consider multiple numeric input standards based upon quantity range.

- Can your numeric fields offer more than one measurement unit? For example, common home lot sizes may be stated in acres or in square feet. If so, you may need select lists to specify the proper units for the numbers. Including select lists will be particularly important if you are dealing with international measurements or currencies.

- Be sure to remind your internal users that not all fields using numeric characters are treated as numbers. Examples include phone numbers and zip codes.

GHOST TEXT

Although a controversial topic among UX professionals, ghost text is a line of instructional copy inside a form field which disappears when the user activates that field and/or begins entering data. Most frequently, ghost text provides a hint regarding the proper response or formatting of input.

Specifications to consider:

- Will your text fields contain ghost text? If so, all fields or only some? If not all fields, what are the rules surrounding its proper use? (For example, it may be used only for input formatting hints such as phone numbers, etc.)

- Provide details on the visual styling for your ghost text: Font, size, style, color and padding.

- Address any accessibility issues.

- Discuss the behavior of your ghost text. If the user begins typing and the ghost text disappears, does it reappear if the user deletes their response and moves to another field? Or does it reappear in blank fields only after a screen refresh?

- If you have other standards that could be used instead of ghost text, such as tool tips or secondary field labels with descriptive information, carefully define which standard should be used under various circumstances and provide cross links.

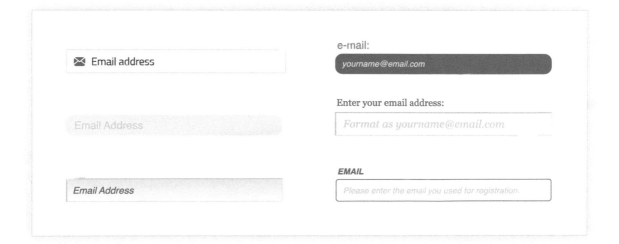

OTHER FORM ELEMENTS

Due to the interactive nature of the web and the unique requirements of each application, countless form patterns have evolved over the years. In this section, I have discussed only the most basic input elements. Below you will find a short list of other input types you may want to consider. But remember to remain vigilant to ensure your framework does not become overwhelming. Scrutinize and challenge each proposed standard to see if it can be combined, simplified, or potentially eliminated.

- Captcha
- Password strength meter
- Auto-Complete
- Credit card type selector
- Speech input
- File upload tool
- Live preview
- Color picker
- Language or country selector

14

ALERTS AND ERRORS

Although everyone tries to design "error-proof" user experiences, invariably things can go wrong. In those instances, you need to clearly and effectively notify your user about the problem. But errors are not the only type of messaging which may be needed on your site. There are many other instances which warrant user notifications—everything from warnings before certain actions are taken to system status updates.

In this section, we will discuss different types of alerts and errors, and explore options for defining their display logic, position, and visual styling.

StyleFramework

Creating Collaborative Style Guides

About   Scaffolding   Elements   Interactions   Navigation   Content   Forms   Alerts|Errors   Fixed Items   Other

Alerts and Errors

Nothing seems to generate quite as much churn and discussion as errors and alerts. While we all agree that UX interfaces should be designed to minimize these errors as much as possible, we must recognize they are sometimes unavoidable. Here is our approved formatting and styling.

Field Level Errors

| User Name | CORRECT |
| Password | INCORRECT |

Valid field entry

Invalid field entry

Treatment and logic for field level validation and errors.

Form Level Errors

We're sorry, there was a problem with your transfer.

Error: Target account not found. Please check the information below and try again.

Visual styling and placement for form level error messages.

Page Level Errors

File Not Found

Oops! Looks like that page has been moved or renamed.

Try using our search function to find what you need:

Visuals and content strategy for page level errors.

No Results Found

Your search - **gazorganplatz recipe** - did not match any documents.

Suggestions:

- Try different keywords.
- Try more general keywords.
- Try fewer keywords.

Content and visual styling when a search generates no matching results.

Confirmation Before Action

You are about to navigate away from OurHypotheticalSite.com.

Content you encounter from this point forward is not determined by, and is not necessarily reflective of the views of, OurHypotheticalSite.com.

Are you sure you wish to proceed?

Yes, Proceed   No Thanks

Treatment and logic for field level validation and errors.

Informational (Non-Error) Alerts

Our Price:

$39.99

$17.99 *Today Only!

Options to communicate non-error messages, such as price updates or urgency.

Leave a Reply

Logged in as Marti Gold. Log out?

Comment

Post Comment

Alerts and Errors Category Landing Page from StyleFramework.com

WHAT TO INCLUDE IN ALERTS AND ERRORS

FIELD LEVEL VALIDATION & ERRORS

Field level validation errors are shown whenever the input to a particular field does not meet a pre-defined requirement or format. This section discusses error messaging that is directly adjacent to individual input fields, and behaviors when performing validation either inline or after hitting submit.

FORM LEVEL ERROR DISPLAYS

Form Level errors occur your the system is unable to process data submitted by a form. This area will define the position and formatting of and positioning of errors or alerts not related to a specific field.

PAGE LEVEL ERRORS

This section will review techniques and options to turn negative page level error messages into a more positive user experience.

NO RESULTS FOUND

Whenever a user enters an open text search string or applies a set of filters to a data set, there is a possibility that no results will be returned. How will your results page handle this situation?

CONFIRMATION BEFORE ACTION

To prevent users from taking inadvertent and perhaps irrevocable or unintended actions, this type of alert can be extremely helpful.

INFORMATIONAL (NON-ERROR) ALERTS

There may be any number of instances where you will need to inform your users about important information. These can range from system status updates to urgency messages such as "five minutes left." Use this section to define these other temporary message formats.

FIELD LEVEL VALIDATION AND ERRORS

There is nothing more frustrating to users than filling out a long form, only to hit submit and have the page reappear with an error. Sadly, technological constraints can sometimes make this situation unavoidable. However, as UX professionals we should always take it upon ourselves to do all we can to alert the user of input problems as soon as they happen.

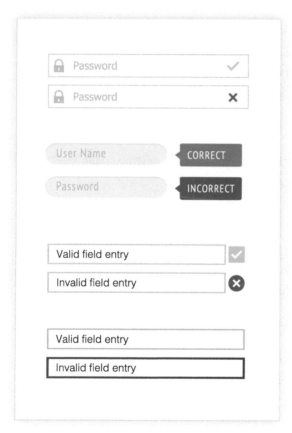

Examples of field level validation and errors.

Specifications to consider:

• Will your forms use inline field validation? Or will the data be validated after the form is submitted?

• If validating inline, present the logic and visual stying for your valid/invalid markers.

• If the form does not validate after submission, will all the fields retain state? Or will certain fields, such as passwords or credit card expiration dates, be cleared?

• If the screen is redrawn after validation, show the messaging and visual treatment to identify the problematic field. Will it change color or add a border? Where will terror description and repair suggestion be presented?

• If the form or copy must shift to accommodate your error messages, show the before and after positioning.

• Give examples of the approved "voice" for your messages. Avoid using negative words as they may make users believe the situation is worse than it is, increasing the risk they will abandon the entire process.

FORM LEVEL ERRORS

In addition to form field errors, you may also need to display error messages that apply to an entire form. These messages are usually more generic in nature and normally appear at the top of the page or form after a forced refresh. But they can provide important information to the user, particularly when an error occurs after submission and all the fields were properly validated.

Specifications to consider:

- Define the display logic for form-level error messages. When should they be displayed? Can you display more than one error at a time?

- Cover the positioning, size and shape of the error messages.

- Discuss any iconography and/or color variations needed to differentiate error types and their severity.

- When a message appears, does your content need to be repositioned or shifted? If possible, include a before and after screen shot.

- Like field error displays, give examples of the approved "voice" for your error messages. Attempt to minimize negative connotations as much as possible and remember to suggest a solution.

Thanks for your interest in our services! For some reason, your information was not submitted to us. Please enter an email address or phone number where we can contact you.

We're sorry, there was a problem with your transfer.

Error: Target account not found. Please check the information below and try again.

The following fields are required: ***E-mail address** ***ZIP Code**

Please complete these fields then retry your submission.

Examples of form level errors.

PAGE LEVEL ERRORS

Often overlooked in style guides, page level errors such as the infamous "404: File Not Found" page occur more frequently than many of us would like. But savvy UX professionals know that a clever "404" or other system error page can turn a potential negative into a brand-building experience. In your UX Style Framework, provide options to address these opportunities.

Specifications to consider:

- Define the "voice" which should be communicated by the error page. Your branding and marketing team will help your owners with this positioning and content. Will your page be humorous? Helpful? Apologetic?

- Will your error pages include your standard global header and/or footer?

- Many sites find it helpful to present open text search functionality. This will permit the user to enter new search terms to locate their desired page. Will that box be pre-populated with terms taken from the user's browsing history?

- As in all error messages, avoid using negative wording or phrases. Encourage the user to stay on your site and use alternative navigation options to find the content they need.

File Not Found

Oops! Looks like that page has been moved or renamed.

Try using our search function to find what you need:

Q

404: Page Not Found

Try checking the URL and trying again.

If you reached this page through a broken link at ThisHypotheticalSite.com, please send an email to admin@thishypotheticalsite.com and let us know about it!

Examples of page level errors.

NO RESULTS FOUND

Whenever a user has the ability to perform an open text search or filter data sets, there is the possibility of returning en empty set of search results. Some companies never want this situation to occur and opt to display "similar" results. Others prefer to deliver precisely what the user requested—even when no results are found. In either event, you should define the logic and display rules for this event.

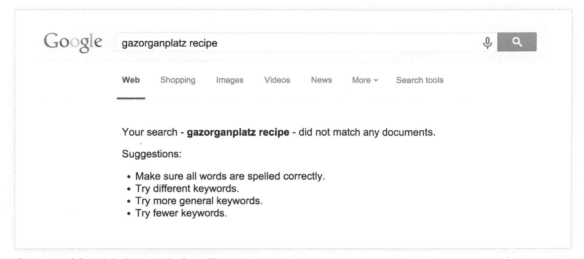

Example of Google's "no results found" page.

Specifications to consider:

- If no exact match results are found, do you want to display "similar results"? If so, how will you label or message those results so the user understands they are not exact matches?

- If you do not wish to display similar results, what message will you show users when no results are found? Provide an example of the copy and its placement.

- Will you present suggestions or hints to broaden the number of potential results?

- If you opt to display both exact matches and similar matches, how will you differentiate between the two? Options to consider include a noticeable break or division between the sets of results, percentage match indicators, or color badges.

CONFIRMATION BEFORE ACTION

Occasionally, you may need your users to confirm an action they have requested before it is carried out, particularly when that action is required, irrevocable, or will take them off your site. Examples of this might include agreeing to terms and conditions, deleting an account, or canceling a reservation. In some industries, confirmation before action notices are a legal requirement before a process is permitted to continue.

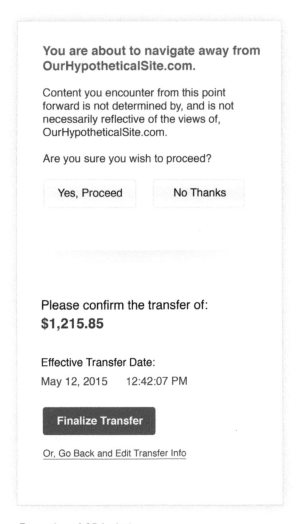

Examples of CBA alerts.

Specifications to consider:

- Clearly define the events which require a confirmation before action alert (CBA). You may find that you have many different categories of CBAs, ranging from a simple, "Are you Sure?" to quite detailed legal copy.

- Once the CBA categories are defined, you can look at the visual styling and presentation for each group. Will the user be required to visit a separate page? Will you display the message in a modal or scroll box?

- Check your proposed visual presentations with your legal department. Some industries do not legal agreements to be displayed inside show-hide interactions.

- Once on the CBA screen, define the user interactions. Will you need both a manual check box as well as the submit button? Or a submit button alone?

- What occurs if the user reaches the CBA screen and realizes he or she does not want to take the action after all? How is the process canceled?

INFORMATIONAL (NON-ERROR) ALERTS

Of course, not every user alert on your site needs to communicate an error. There are many instances where you will need to inform your users of important information or events that can impact their experience. These alerts can range from graphic badges to blocks of text, communicating anything from remaining battery life to urgency messages such as "Only 2 left at this price."

Specifications to consider:

- Define the various alert message types that you will display. Will you include sales or promotional messages in this section or within your content area? Or will all your alerts be limited to non-promotional events such as system status notifications?

- What are the rules governing the display of non-error alerts? You should define the rules about when and where they can appear—otherwise you run the risk of overzealous product managers placing such messages everywhere.

- In most instances, different message types should adopt different visual styling. Include those options here and provide examples. Do not forget links to iconography or images, legal content, nor other assets that may be required.

Our Price:

~~$39.99~~

$17.99   *Today Only!

💬 You have a new offer from Hypothetical Shopping Site! Click here for details.

FREE SHIPPING*
Now Thru 5/31!

*for orders over $50. See More

Examples of simple non-error alerts.

FIXED ITEMS

Although I have emphasized the need to limit your UX Style Framework to individual building block elements, there are a handful of complex components which should also be defined. Standardizing the content and behavior of these components permits users to learn your global site functions quickly. Just as important, they ensure each department is not reinventing the wheel, customizing the UI and code for these complex and repeatable tools.

The fixed items on your site or application may be very specific, and you should address as few of them as possible to ensure your standards continue to evolve. But global headers, footers, login screens, shopping carts and legal text are a few of the components which should be defined here for cross-departmental use.

Screenshot of the Fixed Item Category Landing Page on StyleFramework.com.

WHAT TO INCLUDE IN FIXED ITEMS

HEADERS

Your global headers normally present consistent content, formatting and behaviors site wide. Elements within the header can include your global navigation, a customer personalization area, login links, open-text site search, social media links, etc. While the individual elements within it will adopt standards and patterns defined earlier in this book, its overall layout should be covered here.

FOOTERS

Site or application footers can range from a few lines of text to mini-site maps to full company network link farms. Like the headers, customers often rely upon footers as navigation aides. As a result, they should also be consistent across the site.

LEGAL TEXT

Nearly every site has some type of legally required text. From privacy policies to terms and conditions, these special page or content blocks should be accessible and easily located. In this section, your framework will cover the rules surrounding the display of legal content, along with links to text files containing the current and precise wording required.

SHOPPING CART WIDGET

One of the more complicated persistent widgets on any e-commerce site or application is the shopping cart. While your full-screen checkout path will rely upon interactions defined elsewhere, if you use an 'on-page" widget to show abbreviated descriptions of items in the customer's cart on various pages in your site, its behaviors and styling should be covered here.

LOGIN WIDGET

If your site opts to have a login widget available in multiple locations, it is important to define that functionality here. Login processes are often far more complex than they may appear on the surface.

Again, this list is by no means exhaustive. It is presented to give you an idea of the elements that you might include in your own UX Style Framework.

HEADERS

Whenever a great deal of information is presented in one location, users need a consistent reference point to keep their bearings. This is not limited to site identification, navigation and/or access to frequently used items, but also the need to verify current login status, locate social media links, confirm items in a shopping cart, etc. The goal of your header is for users to feel comfortable when exploring your site, confident they can locate any topic quickly and easily.

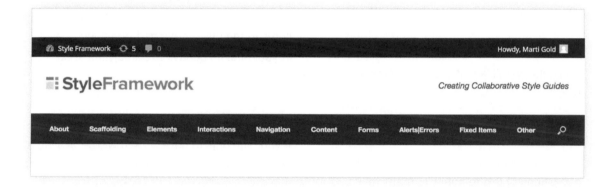

Specifications to consider:

- Will you display multiple header states depending upon the user's current activity? For example, e-commerce sites often present a streamlined header once the customer enters the checkout path in order to minimize distractions. If you use this approach, clearly define the display rules for each variation and provide clear examples.

- Because the global navigation is such an important part of the header, you may find it useful for the headers and global navigation patterns to share owners.

- Responsive sites may have highly complex rules, as headers often change radically depending upon the device being used. Your header page should define all device variations and functionality. Be careful not to include actual breakpoints specifications, but rather cross-reference your "Scaffolding" section.

- Does your header contain personalized information such as customer name? Again, provide all business rules, all necessary dynamic fields, and visual styling.

FOOTERS

Sadly, global footers are often nothing more than an afterthought. If not defined clearly, this useful area can become a poorly organized, inconsistent catch-all for legal disclaimers, links to privacy policies, copyright information, and worst of all SEO spam links. However, if a user reaches the bottom of your page without taking action, you should ask yourself, "What do we want our visitors to do now?" Therefore, your footer should be as carefully considered as your header.

Specifications to consider:

- It is possible to split footers into two sections: A "page variable" and "global fixed" sections. Within the variable section, page creators have the ability to customize the content and make it relevant for a particular page or section. Below that, the global footer can display mutually agreed upon items site wide. This structure addresses footer customization requests as well as minimizing one-off code, as the "variable" area is actually part of the individual page—it is only styled to look like part of the footer. Would this structure benefit your site?

- Users frequently check for particular items in the footer, so it is important to remember recognized conventions. Expected footer content may include: contact us, careers and hiring, privacy policies, FAQs, site maps, email sign up and opt-out links, social media, office locations, terms and conditions, etc.

- Like the header, footer layout and content may vary dramatically from device to device. Provide examples of behaviors and styling for all devices.

LEGAL TEXT

Although legal text could also logically appear in the "Displayed Content" section, I opted to place it here due to its unique nature, the inflexible rules that often surround it, and the need for your framework users to locate this information quickly. It is very important to clearly define the business and presentation rules for all legal text so that designers and QA teams always know precisely how and where to place it.

Privacy notice from Amazon.com

Specifications to consider:

- Will most of your full or multi-page legal text be displayed in a modal or on a separate page? Or will it be split? Modals will keep the user on their current page, and may work best if the user must agree before they are permitted to continue. Stand alone pages may work best if the same terms need to be accessed from many locations or printed.

- Depending upon the use case and regulatory requirements for your industry, legal text might be displayed directly on the page, within a modal, within an accordion or other show-hide interaction. Define the rules and visual styling for all possible options.

- Because the actual legal copy can change quickly, you should always provide reference links to your legal department's most current approved text.

SHOPPING CART WIDGET

Although your checkout path or page will be constructed by combining many of the elements described in previous sections, many sites include a shopping cart widget which presents limited information on selected items and appears on multiple pages. The complexity of coding this type of widget, combined with its restricted space and abbreviated content, requires very clear definitions.

Specifications to consider:

- Will you have a shopping cart widget? Or will clicking any shopping cart icon take you to a stand alone cart page? Using a widget allows your customer to add items and continue shopping without leaving your results pages.

- Will your shopping cart widget be condensed and expand to show full details on click? Will it be persistently displayed (normally in the right navigation)?

- What features will be included or omitted from the widget compared to information shown on your main shopping cart page? What functionality will be included or omitted? For example, can the user change quantities, or delete items directly in the widget?

- How will the shopping cart widget behave on responsive sites? Will the widget be used only for desktop sites, but not tablet or mobile? Be sure to define the business rules, interaction changes, and visual styling for all options.

© jamdesign / Stockfresh

LOGIN WIDGETS

Like the shopping cart, you may opt to funnel all your customers to a single login page. However, you may also decide it is better to have smaller login widgets that can be accessed on demand from various pages. While such login tools may seem simple at first glance, they have an extensive number of use cases and highly varied functionality that can make their layout and coding extremely complex.

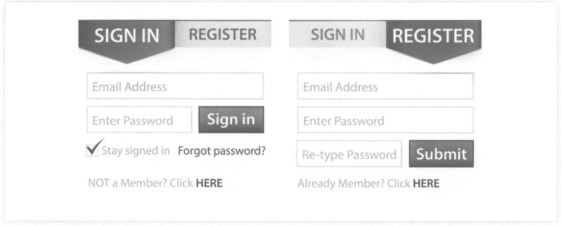

© Liliwhite / Stockfresh

Specifications to consider:

- Will you always funnel users to a stand alone login page (like Amazon.com) or will you have widgets on multiple pages to permit login while in path? Or will you use both?

- Will your login widget be initially hidden and then expanded on click? Or will it be displayed persistently? Will it be accessible from the global header or just at select points within the path?

- What features will be included or omitted from the widget compared to your main login screen? Will users be able to create a new account from the widget? Will they be able to retrieve a lost user name or password? Or will those two instances re-route the user to your stand-alone page?

- Like many other complex elements, the login interaction may need to vary greatly from device to device. Provide business rules and define the behaviors and visual styling for all devices.

16

OTHER ITEMS

This section will present a very specific list of topics that need to be addressed in your framework, yet clearly don't fall into any of the other categories. This section should not become a catch-all for complex, overly prescriptive elements, nor those you simply can't figure out where to place.

For example: Does your site display paid media or advertising? Do you have visual and coding standards for customer emails? While these items may have unique specifications and business rules fully documented in other locations, links to those sources should be included here. Doing so will ensure your UX Style Framework remains your company's primary standards reference source, and never breaks the success guideline "There can be only one."

StyleFramework

Creating Collaborative Style Guides

About   Scaffolding   Elements   Interactions   Navigation   Content   Forms   Alerts|Errors   Fixed Items   Other Items   🔍

Other Items

The holding area for other items which need definition and guidance, but do not fit cleanly into another space. Includes items such as email and mobile application patterns. Great care should be taken before adding items here in order to avoid "item creep" in your Style Framework.

Email Specifications

Information and links on designing and coding emails.

Paid Content & Media

Specifications for advertising and paid content.

SEO Requirements

Best practices and guidelines to improve SEO.

Mobile Applications

Links and information to mobile-app specific standards.

Accessibility

Important information on accessibility requirements.

Leave a Reply

Logged in as Marti Gold. Log out?

Comment

Post Comment

Other Items Category Landing Page from StyleFramework.com.

WHAT TO INCLUDE IN OTHER ITEMS

EMAIL SPECIFICATIONS

Emails often have very strict guidelines for styling and coding. In this section, show examples of approved email designs and provide information on any unique business and technical requirements.

PAID CONTENT & MEDIA GUIDELINES

Many sites include paid or sponsored placements. This could include everything from banner advertising to premium search result placements to paid text links. If your site sells display advertising, you will no doubt run into discrepancies between your grid and standard ad sizes. In this section, you will address those differences, and provide examples of approved ad formats and their placement.

SEO REQUIREMENTS

Very few pages can afford to ignore search engine optimization requirements —an area which is known for its rapid changes. Because of this, SEO departments often create their own guidelines which are updated frequently. Use this section to provide an overview of basic SEO requirements for your designers and developers, and include links to specific technical information on current SEO best practices.

MOBILE APPLICATIONS

In addition to responsive sites, many companies create separate stand-alone mobile applications. While many of the specifications for mobile apps apply across all interactive devices and will included in this document, others are quite specific and should be referenced separately.

ACCESSIBILITY

Due to the importance of accessibility in modern web design, you should strive to address all accessibility requirements for elements and interactions on their respective framework pages. However, general accessibility information and references, such as the location of screen-reader simulators, color contrast checkers, or printed guidelines, should be compiled here.

EMAIL SPECIFICATIONS

Trying to create a consistent HTML email experience across all currently used web-based and dedicated email clients can be challenging at best. Wildly varying rules governing which visual styles will, or will not, be displayed makes effective email design and coding a specialty within many organizations. Use this section to introduce these special considerations, being sure to include links to any offsite documentation that is available.

© magann / Stockfresh

Specifications to consider:

- Does your company create HTML emails? Text only emails? Or both?

- If creating HTML emails, which email clients and web-mail formats do you support?

- Provide basic specifications and visual styling restrictions for designers creating mockups. Maximum width, minimum font sizes, approved media formats, etc.

- Most emails are required to include special disclaimer text that provides a clear unsubscribe link, provides the source of the customers email address, etc. Provide link to the most current text and provide example of the visual styling.

- Do you have a dedicated team that creates and codes your emails? Provide links to their content guidelines for employees who need to create new emails.

PAID CONTENT & MEDIA GUIDELINES

Paid content is often pulled from external networks and will undoubtedly violate many of your scaffolding standards, particularly your grid and modules. Therefore, if your site accepts paid content or media from external sources, you should clearly address those discrepancies here. This is particularly important on responsive sites, as the individual ad sizes, formats, and display rules may need to change from device to device.

Specifications to consider:

- Does your site accept paid content? If so, what types? You may want to define all the different types of paid content first, then break out the details for each in the detailed specification area.

- If your site accepts traditional banner ads, are there restrictions on where those ads may appear? Are the restrictions based on the page type? Position within the page itself? How do they align to the grid? Provide links to your company's detailed media guidelines for the most current information.

- If you accept premium search results, provide visual examples of their formatting for designers creating mockups and prototypes.

- Do you create dedicated landing or advertorial style pages for advertisers? Again, provide links and examples.

- If nothing else, include a link to your company's detailed advertising and media kit so that anyone creating a new page can access the most current guidelines.

© robuart / Stockfresh

SEO GUIDELINES

There is nothing quite so fluid or subject to rapid change as search engine optimization requirements. In order to minimize spamming and insure relevant results for their users, the major search engines update and change their algorithms on a regular basis. Use this page to introduce general SEO best practices, show areas where accessibility and SEO sometimes conflict, and provide an overview of black-hat and gray-hat techniques that must be avoided.

© kbuntu / Stockfresh

Specifications to consider:

- Does your company have a dedicated SEO department or subject matter experts on this topic? If so, one of this pattern's owners should be a representative from that department.

- Be sure to cover techniques that may appear innocent to inexperienced designers or developers, yet are viewed as gray-hat or black-hat practices by the search engines. Touch upon the penalties associated with these practices and their potentially devastating impact on revenue.

- Provide an overview of general SEO best practices for coding, content and design. This will be extremely useful for new designers.

- Have a documented, previously approved process in place for those instances when SEO requests conflict with accessibility requirements. This will ensure that developers and designers know what to do in order to resolve such conflicts quickly.

MOBILE SPECIFIC GUIDELINES

Because mobile application development is such a specialized area, many companies opt to outsource these products. However, even if your mobile apps are built by internal teams, they often incorporate device-specific design and development standards. While these details may be too extensive to cover fully in your UX Style Framework, this page should provide links to all external mobile app standards so your employees can access them when needed.

© ayosphoto / Stockfresh

Specifications to consider:

- Address the different devices that your company currently supports. The introduction of new wearable technologies will expand the need for clear mobile-specific standards.

- Point out any mobile-specific patterns which conflict with responsive standards documented in your framework. Provide information on why the standard has been changed for stand-alone mobile apps.

ACCESSIBILITY

One of the most important areas to address, from social, legal and financial perspectives, is your site's accessibility guidelines. Most companies do not intentionally create inaccessible sites—they are simply unaware they are doing so. Therefore all employees should be aware of the importance and benefits of accessibility compliance, and incorporate these standards into their deliverables.

Specifications to consider:

- Include links to important accessibility resources such as WebAim.org and W3.org so your teams have access to the most recent regulations. These sites often include valuable checklists, analyzers and calculators to help ensure your designs are in compliance. You may also want to include links to educational materials or videos on accessibility best practices for your design and coding teams.

- Discuss the potential legal and public relations consequences to the company if accessibility guidelines are not followed.

- Remind employees that accessibility features also benefit those without disabilities, particularly older users—one of the fastest growing customer segments for many companies.

- Encourage your user research department to include customers with disabilities and create accessibility test scenarios when evaluating site designs and performance.

© carloscastilla / Stockfresh

17

IN CLOSING

In this book, we've challenged many of the core concepts behind a long-standing corporate institution: the style guide. I want to thank you for taking the time to open your mind and revisit a documentation format that has not really changed since the 50s, but is now in dire need of an overhaul.

STILL IN ITS INFANCY...

The idea of a truly dynamic, collaborative style framework is still in its infancy. As more and more UX Style Frameworks and collaborative pattern libraries are created, the items and methods described in this book will evolve. We will learn more about such things as the best overall structure for the framework, the level of detail needed within each pattern, and how our colleagues are effectively using the system.

The key point is that in a world where agile methodologies and truly innovative devices are making new interface designs common, static standards documentation is becoming a relic of the past. The time has come for our style guides and pattern libraries to evolve and change, because the sites and applications they define are evolving and changing.

Even if you can't adopt a full UX Style Framework right away, implementing even a few of the changes proposed in this book will prolong the life of your standards and improve consistency on your site.

We welcome your input at StyleFramework. com and hope that you will contribute to the community's discussion of this topic. Ideally, we will build a gallery of links to various UX Style Frameworks, along with a knowledge base of best practices generated by industry professionals like yourself. Please feel free to check Styleframework.com and follow us on social media for the latest information on this topic.

Site: www.styleframework.com
Twitter: @martigold and @styleframework

SUPPLEMENTAL MATERIALS

A

APPENDIX

COMMON
ELEMENTS
CHART

I started my research by creating a list of the UI elements and interactions defined in the popular presentation layer coding framework, Bootstrap. I expanded the Bootstrap list with other common elements and interaction patterns appearing in additional publicly available sources, and ended up with a list of 124 core elements, interactions, and content formats. The additional items were taken from representative samples of online brand/style guides, UX pattern libraries, and development code repositories from well-known corporations including Expedia, Bank of America, AT&T, Dell, Microsoft, and Apple. I also referenced material from online UI resources such as the Yahoo Pattern Library.

I put three column headings on the chart: one for Marketing Style Guides; a second for UX Pattern Libraries; and a third for Development Code Repositories. Then I began adding squares — placing a bright orange square in the corresponding column when any element was regularly included in that particular document type. I used a gray square if the element was regularly included, but only partially defined. The result of that analysis is shown on the following pages.

Element Name	Online Style Guide *Marketing*	Pattern Library *UX*	Component Library *Development*
Layout			
Grid system	■	■	■
Baseline grid (to set vertical rhythm)	■	■	■
Container Styling	■	■	■
Margins and Padding	■	■	■
Global Visuals			
Logos and their proper use	■	■	
Colors	■	■	■
Iconography	■	■	■
Sprites			■
Region/culture indicators (US, GB, FR, etc.)	■	■	■
Visiblity classes (based on viewport size)			■
Content Styling			
Photography Style	■	■	
Illustration Styles	■	■	
Punctuation Guides	■	■	
Capitalization Rules	■	■	■
Abbreviation Rules	■	■	
Hypenation Rules	■	■	■
Buttons			
Primary buttons	■	■	■
Cancel buttons	■	■	■
Disabled buttons	■	■	■
Icon buttons (no text)	■	■	■
Button with counter	■	■	■
Switch (on/off) or toggle		■	■

Element Name	Online Style Guide *Marketing*	Pattern Library *UX*	Component Library *Development*
Typography			
Font Families	■	■	■
Font base size	■	■	■
Font weights	■	■	■
Emphasis or italic	■	■	■
Text alignment	■	■	■
Headings	■	■	■
Subheadings	■	■	■
Body copy (Paragraph) styles	■	■	■
Captions	■	■	■
Unordered lists	■	■	■
Ordered lists	■	■	■
Unstyled lists	■	■	■
Pull quotes	■	■	■
Drop capitals	■	■	■
Subscript and superscript	■	■	■
Disclaimer Text	■	■	■
Special Formatting			
Links	■	■	■
Horizontal rules	■	■	■
Time	■	■	■
Addresses	■	■	■
Phone numbers	■	■	■
Currency	■	■	■
Dates	■	■	■
Other common formats (SSN, discounts, etc.)	■	■	■
Tables	■	■	■
Charts	■	■	■
Arrows	■	■	■
White space characters			■

Element Name	Online Style Guide *Marketing*	Pattern Library *UX*	Component Library *Development*
Forms			
Form Field Design	■	■	■
Form Field Label design	■	■	■
Form Field Label position	■	■	■
Text input field	■	■	■
Email input field		■	■
Number input field		■	■
URL input field		■	■
Color input field		■	■
Range input (or sliders)	■	■	■
Date input (calendar display/interaction)	■	■	■
Search input (often with submit button)		■	■
Search suggestions dropdown		■	■
Phone input		■	■
Password input		■	■
Scrolling Text area formatting	■	■	■
Checkboxes	■	■	■
Radio buttons	■	■	■
File input		■	■
Select menu (dropdowns)	■	■	■
Required field indicator (*)	■	■	■
Money amount entry form		■	■
Form help text or note		■	■
Input field validation states			■
Input size variations		■	■
Amount selector		■	■
Currency selector		■	■
Payment method selector (credit cards)	■	■	■
Speech recognition input		■	■

Element Name	Online Style Guide *Marketing*	Pattern Library *UX*	Component Library *Development*
Navigation			
Breadcrumbs	■	■	■
Footer navigation (usually text links)	■	■	■
Tabbed panels	■	■	■
Horizontal Nav formatting (usually global or top)	■	■	■
Vertical Nav formatting (often down left side)	■	■	■
Pagination	■	■	■
Subnavigation (dropdowns/flyouts)	■	■	■
Toggle (nav collapses at small resolutions to single button)		■	■
Interaction elements			
Alerts or notifications	■	■	■
Progress bars	■	■	■
Activity/loading Indicators (aka "spinner")	■	■	■
Tooltips or flyouts	■	■	■
Modal, dialog or lightbox	■	■	■
Expand a section	■	■	■
Contract or Collapse a section	■	■	■
Accordion panels	■	■	■
Animations	■	■	
Skip links (scroll to elements in-page)			■
Code Elements			
Code snippets (CSS, HTML. Javascript)		■	■
Code comments			■
Variables			■
Sample output		■	■
Tables			
Individual cell formatting	■	■	■
Headings	■	■	■
Row styling	■	■	■

Element Name	Online Style Guide *Marketing*	Pattern Library *UX*	Component Library *Development*
Column styling	■	■	■
Disclaimers or notes		■	■
Complex Components or Pages			
Audio players	■	■	■
Blog page formatting	■	■	
Carousel or image slider	■	■	■
Credit Card Selector		■	■
Comments/discussion formatting		■	■
FAQs	■	■	■
Footnotes	■	■	■
Hero or promo layouts	■	■	
Landing pages	■	■	
Lists with thumbnails or images	■	■	■
Maps	■	■	■
Meta data			■
Off Canvas modules		■	■
Page header	■	■	■
Photo gallery	■	■	■
Progress indicators (e.g. shopping cart steps)	■	■	■
Shopping cart design	■	■	■
Statistics (numbers with labels)	■	■	■
Tags or keywords (cloud or list)		■	■
Video players	■	■	■

Total Items	124
Items in all three columns	84
Items in two of the three columns	32
Items that appeared in a single source	8
Percentage overlap	93.5%

INDEX

T - #0759 - 101024 - C244 - 235/191/11 [13] - CB - 9781138856479 - Gloss Lamination